More Advance Praise **Child**

"As a parent-cum-profess_____ ... the autism field for over 45 years, I applaud the energy and wisdom Peggy Lou Morgan has put into this book. I believe the best success comes when parents assume professionals *want* to help, even if they don't yet know how. Such partnerships produce most of the best success stories in the field of autism. Ms. Morgan is not only a skilled writer, but also a good storyteller. Her book should be a welcomed addition to the autism literature."

> —Ruth Christ Sullivan, Ph.D., Founder, Executive Director of Autism Services Center; First President of Autism Society of America (1968–1970); author, lecturer, activist, parent

"This book is written from the heart. It presents an honest and open view of some of the many struggles encountered by the parents of highly challenging students with disabilities. In her book *Parenting Your Complex Child* Peggy Morgan shares some of these struggles, which include those with schools, doctors, social situations, and more. She presents an honest reflection of her own frustrations and fears and shares a solution-focused perspective that proved successful.

"Parents who are experiencing serious challenges in advocating on behalf of their challenging child should read this book. Reading between the lines and finding the out-of-the-ordinary philosophical approach to partnerships between parents and those who provide services and supports allows parents and professionals alike to look at how they work together. Ms. Morgan reminds us all to keep the focus of our efforts on the child and to maintain good working relationships in the face of adversity and differences. She is right!"

> —Heidi Schack, Director, Special Services, Silver Falls School District, 210 East C Street, Silverton, OR 97381; Master's of Science in Education and Standard Licensure in Special Education and School Administration

"Peggy Morgan provides us with a touching, sincere account of [her son] Billy Ray's life . . . a most accurate, invaluable resource, as well, for families facing the constant challenge of dealing with profoundly developmentally challenged children/young adults."

> —Ed Ruden, M.D.

"Peggy Morgan gives a compelling firsthand account of the challenges of raising a child with a developmental disability. She provides a unique perspective on how to advocate for your child when the solutions seem out of reach. Great way to make a difference with other parents who are struggling with similar challenges!"

—Mary Lynn O'Brien, Developmental Pediatrician and Board Member, NW Autism Foundation

PARENTING YOUR COMPLEX CHILD

PARENTING YOUR
COMPLEX CHILD

*Become a Powerful Advocate for the Autistic,
Down Syndrome, PDD, Bipolar,
or Other Special-Needs Child*

Peggy Lou Morgan

AMACOM AMERICAN MANAGEMENT ASSOCIATION

New York ■ Atlanta ■ Brussels ■ Chicago ■ Mexico City ■ San Francisco
Shanghai ■ Tokyo ■ Toronto ■ Washington, D.C.

Special discounts on bulk quantities of AMACOM books are available to corporations, professional associations, and other organizations. For details, contact Special Sales Department, AMACOM, a division of American Management Association, 1601 Broadway, New York, NY 10019.
Tel.: 212-903-8316. Fax: 212-903-8083.
Website: www.amacombooks.org

This publication is designed to provide accurate and authoritative information in regard to the subject matter covered. It is sold with the understanding that the publisher is not engaged in rendering legal, accounting, or other professional service. If legal advice or other expert assistance is required, the services of a competent professional person should be sought.

Various names used by companies to distinguish their software and other products can be claimed as trademarks. AMACOM uses such names throughout this book for editorial purposes only, with no intention of trademark violation. All such software or product names are in initial capital letters or ALL CAPITAL letters. Individual companies should be contacted for complete information regarding trademarks and registration.

Library of Congress Cataloging-in-Publication Data

Morgan, Peggy Lou, 1950–
    Parenting your complex child : become a powerful advocate for the autistic, Down syndrome, PDD, bipolar, or other special-needs child / Peggy Lou Morgan.
        p.   cm.
    Includes index.
    ISBN-10: 0-8144-7316-4 (pbk.)
    ISBN-13: 978-0-8144-7316-0
    1. Developmentally disabled children—Care.   2. Developmentally disabled children—Services for.   3. Parents of children with disabilities—Attitudes.
    4. Parents of children with disabilities—Psychology.   5. Parenting—Psychological aspects.   6. Communication in the family.   I. Title.
    HV891.M73   2006
    649'.15—dc22   2005032514

Printing number

10 9 8 7 6 5 4 3 2 1

To Billy Ray,
who has trained his Mommie so well,

———————————— *and* ————————————

to Ronald R. Roy, M.D. ("Dr. Ron"), deceased.
Dr. Ron's words, "If only the world could understand you through your Mom's ears and eyes," still ring in my ears as a motivating force to communicate Billy Ray to his world.

CONTENTS

FOREWORD

AS A CLINICAL GENETIC COUNSELOR, I can sometimes help diagnose a condition or guide families to resources after a diagnosis. What I can't do is tell families what life is like when you raise a child with special needs. This book offers excellent descriptions of day-to-day life when parenting a complex child.

Its descriptions are valuable not only for parents, but also for any professional working with them (clinician, social service agency worker, teacher, day care provider, etc). It is too easy for professionals to forget how complicated life can be for the parent of a special-needs child. When more than one special need is present in the child, the difficulties don't just add up—they can multiply many times over. Peggy Lou Morgan's vivid account of her experience helps us understand the amazing job performed each day as a "complex parent."

One of my favorite parts of this book is the idea that you can create a life for your complex child. Ms. Morgan describes many small combat zones at home, at school, and out in public. I like how she describes those challenges, and how she finally transcended the view that the world was at war with her. I have often seen parents in clinic who view the world as a battlefield, but who never arrive at a "peace plan." Ms. Morgan's peace plan—to build a safe world along with willing, informed colleagues—is a new concept to me. This vision is unique among the parents

I've come to know. I hope others can learn from her experiences to build a community for their own children.

Perhaps the most valuable parts of this book are Ms. Morgan's suggestions for observing and keeping records. Medical researchers don't study many complex children. As health-care providers, we depend on the published research to inform us so we may provide advice and guidance to families. If a patient is "complex," and doesn't fit the description of a single condition described in the research literature, we are left with little to share. Teaching parents to observe and problem-solve empowers them to fill in the information gaps for themselves.

This book is so much more than a list of suggested responses to particular behaviors. It's a detailed guide to understanding your child and building a place in the world for him or her from the ground up. Truly an amazing feat by any measure.

Kate Crow, MS, CGC
Genetic Counselor, Kaiser Permanente Genetics

LIFE WITH A COMPLEX developmentally disabled child is like a war with many battlefields.

Battlefield one: Your own home can feel like a combat zone. Your child may be agitated because of frustration over being in inappropriate programs in school or with his schedules at home and away. He may be confused about what is expected of him. He may not know what he is going to do next, so he is worrying about it. He may sense the tension you feel about trying to get help for him. He does not know why you are upset. He may be agitated, destructive, and aggressive. When your child is uncomfortable with school or other problems, it influences his behavior and puts stress on the whole family. He may sleep poorly, so both you and your child live your lives sleep deprived. There is little peace in the home for anyone.

Battlefield two: Dealing with schools and agencies to obtain the services and programs your child needs can turn into a drawn-out source of conflict. These services are mandated by laws, but parents often have problems getting schools and agencies to provide the services the parents believe are appropriate. Also, these schools and agencies are not necessarily funded sufficiently. Parents try to prove their children's eligibility for specific services, while schools and agencies cautiously protect their budgets.

Advocating is the buzzword—and it is crucial that you become a powerful and knowledgeable advocate for your child. However, some parents see this as a combat order. The general attitude in numerous e-mails I receive and conversations with parents is that you need to be a powerful opponent, to "kick butt" and "win," or to sue the authorities. It is like declaring war between the professionals and programs expected to educate or provide services to your child and the most important person(s) in her life, you, her parents. The real victim when this situation occurs is your child.

Battlefield three: Going out in public can be like walking into a firefight. The laws granting equal access control only what businesses must do, not how other people must act. People stare or make hurtful comments, which can agitate the child, bring on inappropriate behaviors, and cause you to become upset. The more upset you are, the more your child picks up on it. Everywhere you take your child can turn into a struggle. Slow waiters or grocery clerks, too many displays in the store, etc., can affect his behavior.

WHAT THIS BOOK WILL DO FOR YOU

Parenting Your Complex Child is a bit like a peace plan aimed at helping you reduce the conflict surrounding you and your child. Yes, this book talks about advocating too, but from a different point of view. To me, advocating does not mean drawing battle lines and digging in for a fight to the finish. I believe that advocating becomes easier when you are able to communicate and demonstrate how your child really is rather than arguing or becoming a skilled presenter. It is about team building and mutual understanding of a child's needs.

In part one, we will look at the real world in which you and your complex child live. Part two will help you learn from your child by reading his behaviors and responses, not just what he verbalizes. The key concepts here are communicating and adapting. You will learn to:

- Communicate with your child in whatever way works best for him

- Adapt his life to what works best for him and you

- Communicate to others in his world what he needs and how he functions best

In chapter 15 I will talk about training caregivers when needed so that they maintain consistency with the plan you have created for your child. Chapter 16 helps ensure that the dream you have created for your child will continue after you are no longer able to take care of him.

The ideas discussed in this book will help you as the parent of a child with behavior disorders, developmental problems, and mental-health diagnoses such as autism, Down syndrome, bipolar disorder, schizophrenia, attention deficit hyperactivity disorder (ADHD), pervasive developmental disorder (PDD), and others. These approaches are not designed for any specific disorder or combination of disorders. I tell my son's story through my experiences and then discuss what has worked for me. I believe they will work for you, too, whatever your circumstances.

Parenting Your Complex Child is not based on diagnosis, and I will not provide specific methods for working with your child. This book is based on my experiences with my complex child, Billy Ray. No matter what the diagnosis, your child is a unique individual. Your approach must be based on his or her individual needs. The suggestions in the book will help you become an expert on your child and thereby become the rightful leader of his or her team. It will teach you how to decide what works best for your own child and advocate for that.

If this sounds like work, it will be in the beginning. However, when your child is more comfortable with his life at home and at school, and you are working as a team with the professionals involved in his care, you will realize how much easier life has become.

Peggy Lou Morgan
www.parentingyourcomplexchild.com
www.lighthouseparents.com
http://parentingacomplexchild.blogspot.com

——— A C K N O W L E D G M E N T S ———

THERE ARE SO MANY PEOPLE who have provided support and encouragement along the way in developing the methods that are contained herein. It would be impossible to list them all. Know that each one has been valuable.

Dr. Mary Lynn O'Brien, our developmental pediatrician for eighteen years, has been there for Billy Ray and me through many crises and when the "dumb-parent treatment" wore me down on other fronts.

I don't know where to start thanking Dr. Edward Ruden, our pediatrician since Dr. O'Brien's retirement. Dr. Ruden listened to my concerns and helped work through problems for Billy Ray. During a three-year period of physical illness when I thought we would lose Billy Ray to infections and medication side effects, Dr. Ruden hung in there with us. There is a picture on Billy Ray's computer screen saver that shows how healthy he has become. I think, "Thank God for Dr. Ruden," every time I see it.

This book would not have happened without my literary agent, William Brown, Waterside Productions, who gently made suggestions, kept me focused, and encouraged me. I thank him regularly for finding me the best editor, Ellen Kadin of AMACOM Books, any first-time author could ever have. Ellen's patience and understanding in explaining the publishing process helped so much. The whole team at AMACOM has been wonderful to work with. I can't thank Barry Richardson enough for his editing and the confidence he gave me in my work. Thank you to Erika Spelman, who had to put up with my lack of experience with publishing details and numerous questions.

The most important thanks is to Billy Ray, from whom I have learned so much just by watching him. I also want to thank my husband, Larry Morgan, who has assisted by helping with Billy Ray and doing Internet research. The support and encouragement of friends and family gave me strength to stay with this project. I want to especially mention my mother-in-law, Luci Green, who has been a constant support. I am honored to have her as mother-in-law. My parents, Ron and Daisy Waterhouse, for helping get Lighthouse Parents started and for their encouragement. Even at fiftyish, it is so important to know Daddy is proud of his little girl.

Billy Ray and I have been blessed by marrying into a large family. Larry's four adult children and twelve grandchildren have touched Billy Ray's life and mine. I couldn't possibily relate the ways each has contributed. Mark and Michael Morgan, my stepsons, have played with Billy Ray and given him a chance to be a real boy. I want to thank Michael and his wife, Rebecca, for the effort it has taken to ensure that we really get to know his children, Elora, Alena, Hans, and Oren. As result of their contact with Billy Ray, I have learned how to communicate Billy Ray to other children so that a relationship was possible. Their responses to Billy Ray helped me to create community activities that were more comfortable for him and for his community. Michael's involving Billy Ray in activities with his boys, so that I could have quality time with Elora, Alena, and Rebecca, has been renewing in ways that I couldn't possibly explain. I want to thank my daughter-in-law Rebecca Perez-Morgan for helping me to see things from a teacher's perspective and for helping me review the editing that came in during Billy Ray's hospitalization. Thanks also to Mark who has reviewed and made suggestions about the website and has been an encouragement to me.

Heidi Schack was at one point the director of special education who was ultimately responsible for Billy Ray's education. We have disagreed, negotiated, and learned from each other. Now that Billy Ray is no longer in school, Heidi is my good friend. She made time to review a draft of this manuscript, gave me valuable feedback, and served as reviewer.

Thanks to Kevin Loyd, who served as caregiving assistant during a substantial period while I was experimenting with what worked for Billy Ray. His skill with animals was so helpful in training one of Billy Ray's service dogs. During Billy Ray's illness, Larry and I would have never gotten out if not for Kevin, the only person we trusted with Billy Ray. Thanks also for all the grilled cheese sandwiches you slipped in front of the monitor when I was pounding away on this manuscript.

Thanks to the Reverend Ray Jones, who has been my pastor, friend, and sometimes literary adviser. Thanks also to the Reverend Bud Pugh and the Reverend Nathan Covington, who have provided encouragement and prayer support despite their busy schedules. I do not want to forget our current pastor, the Reverend Richard Lighthill, a great pastor who has offered great support while we dealt with both moving and trying to finish this book. He even makes a mean Crock-Pot meal.

PART ONE

THE JOURNEY
Life with a Complex Child

LIFE WITH A COMPLEX CHILD is not "usual."
Finding understanding is perhaps the most difficult part
of parenting a complex child. Working with those you
expect to understand most may be more frustrating than
working with your child.

CHAPTER

1

THE COMPLEX CHILD

THERE IS NOTHING PROFOUND in the use of the term *complex child*. I selected it because I feel the terms *challenging child* and *complicated child*—in the literature regarding developmental disabilities that I have read—are overused and may not demonstrate the type of child I am trying to describe. Since I have started using the term, I have seen autism described as "a complex developmental disability." The term as I use it could certainly describe some children with autism but is not limited by diagnosis.

Complex child is used here to describe a child whose behavior and responses to treatment are so challenging that he (or she) is often described by doctors, educators, and social-work professionals as "one of the most complicated patients (or clients) I have ever worked with." He may experience some form of autism, a conduct or behavior disorder, or a variety of other developmental disabilities. He may have multiple labels (diagnoses), including mental-illness labels. He is probably more complicated than other children with the same diagnoses tend to be. He may fail to fit exactly into one diagnosis. The symptoms he experiences may be different from most children within the same diagnoses, and/or he fails to respond to medications, behavior modification, or educational approaches the way other children do.

It is not my intention that the term *complex child* implies anything about intelligence or level of functioning. Ability to function or perform at certain levels socially, educationally, or in the degree of self care is often dependent on many variables. Programs or other things in the environment that confuse a child can bring out behavior that makes the child appear to be much lower functioning. It is my strong belief that many complex children are so frustrated with trying to be understood that their behavior disguises strengths and intelligence. There are many children presumed to be low functioning who can amaze the world with their capabilities when allowed to demonstrate them in the way they need to.

Lest you think this book is only for parents of complex children, I would like to share a little of my son's story. (I will go into much more detail in chapter 2.) Billy Ray has been two types of child in one short lifetime. There have always been some challenges dealing with his behavior, school issues, medical and psychiatric care, etc.

Billy Ray developed fairly quickly following his adoptive placement at fifteen months old with Raymond, my late husband, and me. He was able to be stabilized on medications for a number of years despite his experience of Down syndrome, attention deficit hyperactivity disorder (ADHD), and bipolar disorder as well as physical issues from time to time. He was very socially acceptable and able to do many things, some of which could be considered high functioning. I was able to create a business around his care. At age twelve, he also handled the death of his adoptive father remarkably well.

At fourteen years old Billy Ray suffered a series of seizures believed to be caused by a medication reaction. His personality changed permanently at that point. He became a complex child. I had to learn from Billy Ray all over again. His way of seeing things or reasoning changed entirely. For a time, the once high-functioning child (who could feed himself except for cutting his meat, take a bath independently, and do many activities on his own) disappeared completely. For a while Billy Ray had to be fed and cared for much as an infant. I thought he would never be able to do any of the things he was capable of before. Instead of returning to what was normal for him before the seizures, the way most children do within six months of such events, Billy Ray began developing increasing symptoms of autism. The good news is that once we struggled to understand things from his perspective, some of the high-functioning skills returned.

SOME CHARACTERISTICS OF THE COMPLEX CHILD

The old joke about children not coming with an instruction manual is never truer than in the case of a complex child. Traditional parenting approaches simply do not work if you can't reason with him or he can't understand consequences. You are looking for guidance to show you how to parent and provide appropriate care and education. Some form of label or diagnosis generally triggers this guidance. However, because more than one professional is generally involved, and they may disagree regarding diagnoses, it is harder for parents of complex children to find support or guidance.

A complex child seems to be the exception to every rule. When the doctor states what children "usually" experience, it might be very different from what your complex child experiences. It would be difficult to give a description that would fit all complex children, but here, based on my son, Billy Ray, and my observance of others, is a partial glimpse into what I see as a complex child:

- Reasoning with the complex child is difficult or impossible because he may not see things in ways that seem logical to you. He may fail to understand "no" or "wait" and rarely accepts "I don't know" for an answer.

- The complex child is easily frustrated, agitated, or confused. Out of that frustration or confusion may come aggression, property destruction, or other negative behaviors.

- A complex child's aggression can range from minor punches to dangerous attacks. Property destruction can range from breaking a trinket to throwing furniture, punching holes in walls, breaking windows, etc.

- His behavior is unpredictable and hard to manage. He can seem like a spoiled child rather than someone with a disability. Neither behavior modification approaches nor medications seem to work in the long term.

- His behavior can be cyclic: He is able to communicate his needs and functions on a high level one time, only to become "stuck" and frustrated the next.

- A complex child is able to focus only on his own needs and wants. He sees others as extensions of himself. For example, if you are Mom, the child thinks your sole purpose is to take care of him. Your job is to meet his every need. Absent that, he can become frustrated and/or aggressive. He is less likely to see Mom as a separate entity to relate to or someone with individual needs.

- A complex child refuses to be pushed into existing programs or systems; he needs an entire life (school, community, and home) designed specifically for him.

- A complex child may seem off in his own little world, and the things he says have nothing to do with reality. You may wonder if your child hears voices in his head, but he is not able to tell you what he experiences.

- A complex child may ask the same questions repeatedly, even in the middle of the night. Often he creates an answer and will not allow the answer to be variable. For example, one of Billy Ray's stepbrothers, "Bubba Mike," was deployed for Operation Iraqi Freedom. We tried to tell Billy Ray that Bubba was in the army and explain what that meant. For months, he refused to accept it. Then Michael sent us some pictures of himself in full military attire, and Billy Ray changed his answer to "he's in the army." However, after Michael returned home from Iraq, Billy Ray did not want to accept that "he's in California where he lives" (the old answer) until after Michael visited a few months later.

- The complex child may have illogical fetishes about clothes or possessions. He may even name them. This can get confusing, especially if he has many similar items. For example, Billy Ray somehow identified his beloved high school principal, Mr. Koger, with slacks and white shirts. He calls his own white Western shirts "Koger shirts," and we had to sort through every white shirt in the closet to find his Koger shirt. I finally discovered the way he identified this shirt from other seemingly identical shirts: There was a burgundy-colored strip across the label. If that burgundy strip is absent, it is not a Koger shirt. For a while, "Koger slacks" were Billy Ray's black Western slacks, but then blue slacks became Koger slacks without notice to this confused Mom.

- The complex child may be verbal or nonverbal but does not respond to verbal cues consistently. He may need visual cues to respond.

DIFFICULTIES IN PARENTING THE COMPLEX CHILD

Because of the many challenges, the parents of a complex child experience more difficulty in their day-to-day lives and receive less understanding and support than the average parents of less severely impacted special-needs children. Figure 1.1 makes just a few comparisons among parenting an average child, a less severely impacted developmentally disabled child, and a complex child. Please note that physical disabilities were not specially considered in these comparisons and would increase the impact on parents if present.

I started laughingly using the term *illogical care* based on multiple discussions (sometimes heated) I have had with my present husband about his stepson. Larry, the father of four grown children, is a bright and logical person. His parenting advice, before Billy Ray's changed personality, was reasonable and worked with Billy Ray, who experienced Down syndrome, ADHD, and bipolar disorder. However, those same approaches do not often work with Billy Ray now that he experiences the additional autistic-like symptoms such as communication problems, frequent inability to focus, irritability, aggression, and inability to put things into words.

(text continued on page 11)

FIGURE 1.1 Comparing children.

Average Children	Less Impacted Developmentally Disabled Children	Complex Developmentally Disabled Children
Routine colds, flu, and immunization visits to the doctor.	Routine colds, flu, and immunization visits to the doctor. More visits to check on status and ensure child is progressing. Child may have some immune-system issues, which may require more frequent medical care.	Routine colds, flu, and immunization visits to the doctor. More visits to check on status and ensure child is progressing. Child may have some immune-system issues, which may require more frequent medical care. Regular visits to pediatrician and/or psychiatrist or neurologist to monitor behavior. Generally fighting a balancing act with medications required to make child at least manageable at home and school. Constant concern about side effects if medication is used. Sometimes psychologist, play therapist, or in-home behavior therapist services require many meetings or appointments.
Parent conferences at school during scheduled time each year and occasionally for problems that come up.	Individual Education Plan (IEP) team meetings at least yearly. Sometimes more than one a year if there are learning or other problems to be monitored.	IEP meetings generally at least twice a year, and in the most difficult cases, quarterly or even monthly. Puts strain on employment of parents.

Review report cards or progress notes that come home or in the mail.	Can experience "dumb-parent treatment" when parent requests pushing the child to achieve more. Frequent contact with the teacher or aides to follow up on child's goals and needs.	Parents may experience the dumb-parent treatment when trying to assert that the child's potential is higher than the educational professionals see it—this is especially true if it requires more work or funds on the part of the school district. Regular or even constant contact with the teacher or aides regarding problems in school or to schedule meetings. Not only frustrating for the parent, but creates problems with trying to maintain employment.
Most children can go to friends or family while parents are out for evening or on vacation. Most children are able to be cared for by responsible teenagers for an evening.	Harder for parents to find a sitter—child needs closer supervision. Some children can stay with teen sitters, most stay with family, depending on physical health. Some attend respite-care centers.	Need specially trained care providers, who are very expensive and difficult to find. Respite centers might not work because of behaviors.
Day care is expensive and a challenge to find, but can usually be found.	Day care is more difficult to find because of the child's needs, but usually possible. Child will experience more problems than "normal" kids in day care but usually tolerates it pretty well.	Day care programs extremely difficult to find for child with behavior issues. Child often kicked out of programs, leaving the parents with no care, putting strain on the child and the parents' employment. This affects ability to support the child and provide medical insurance. In-home staff frequently undependable and sometimes performance issues are a problem.

(continues)

FIGURE 1.1 Continued.

Average Children	Less Impacted Developmentally Disabled Children	Complex Developmentally Disabled Children
Sometimes difficult to get child to stay in bed or sleep by himself in the early years, but generally sleeps several hours a night once asleep.	Sleep may be more of an issue but generally able to tolerate sleep medications so parent and child get some sleep.	Sleep often a constant problem. Medications may not work or, at least, child builds up tolerance to them within a few weeks or months. Parents awaken many times in the night. Parents live their lives sleep deprived, which affects every area of their lives. Kids often nap during the day while parents must work. Parents sometimes end up sleeping with the child or being in his room—major impact on marriages. Parent may take desperate measures, such as sleeping with one arm over a bouncing, giggly child and dozing because you can't stay awake another minute, or putting a sleeping bag in child's doorway so you will know if he tries to escape from his room.
All children are a strain on parents financially, especially with the cost of good day care and other activities children become involved in such as sports and scouting.	More expensive than most children, especially if there are medical problems and child care costs more than for average children.	Very expensive, usually more medical copayments and items not covered by insurance or state health plans, increased clothing needs, higher costs of child care. Sometimes requires one parent to stay home, because affordable care is not possible. Even if governmental funding for in-home staff is available, finding appropriate staff not always possible.

ADOPTING INDIVIDUALIZED APPROACHES

The idea of needing to understand, from a child's perspective, whether his requests or behaviors appear logical to us or not, extends to every area of his life, not just to parenting. When we can understand, even in part, where the child is coming from, we can respond more appropriately to him and try to prevent reoccurrence or at least minimize the degree of the negative behavior when it does reoccur.

You try to teach your child to act in acceptable ways by using parenting methods that you are familiar with and then wonder why they do not work. Chances are you are frustrated not only by your child's lack of responsiveness to your parenting but also by all the well-meaning parenting advice you get from numerous sources.

I read everything I could on parenting developmentally disabled children and even reread *The Strong-Willed Child: Birth Through Adolescence* by Dr. James Dobson (Tyndale House Publishers, 1978). Nothing worked since the change in Billy Ray. It was a difficult adjustment because he had been a much easier child to parent before his medication reaction at age fourteen.

Little by little I began to understand more of his thinking processes and anticipate behaviors. I also realized that I was making the problem worse when I tried to use traditional parenting approaches. He needed an individualized approach.

Figure 1.2 compares how a few different parenting approaches might be appropriate for an average child, a less impacted developmentally disabled child, and a complex child. I have by no means listed all behaviors or responses, but I think you will get the idea that it is important to adapt your approaches to meet your child's ability to respond.

Your child may respond to things differently than Billy Ray. I share the insights to show you how I have learned what worked for Billy Ray. I want you to be able to figure out what works for your child, not do things just because they worked for my son. You will understand your own child more as you start to use the ideas in chapter 8, "The Best Teacher—Your Child."

With this partial glimpse into a complex child, you should realize that you are not alone in facing these challenges, however individualized your child's circumstances may be. There is much hope. You can make

(*text continued on page 16*)

FIGURE 1.2 Comparison of parenting approaches.

Behavior	Potential Response by Parent to Average Child	Potential Response by Parent to Less Impacted Developmentally Disabled Child	Potential Response to Complex Developmentally Disabled Child
Intentionally spilling or throwing food or some minor property destruction.	Clean up mess and time-out would be one response. Withdrawal of privileges, etc. might also be considered.	Clean up the mess and, if you felt the child could understand what was done, some consequences such as time-out or withdrawal of privileges.	Attempt to have child clean up the mess. However, he can get stuck in the behavior and continue behavior if it is out of confusion or frustration to communicate something to parent or caregiver. It is necessary to tread more lightly than with other children. If he does get stuck you may need to use other methods for responding to aggression (below).
Aggression toward another person.	Ask the child to say "I'm sorry." Discuss the unacceptable behavior with the child and impose some form of reasonable consequence.	Ask the child to say "I'm sorry." Discuss the unacceptable behavior with the child and impose some form of consequence appropriate for the child's functioning level.	First, block the aggressive behavior to protect child and victim. Depending on the child's normal response, asking her to say "I'm sorry" can bring about intense guilt, which makes the problem worse instead of being an appropriate response.

Often a child hates the behavior as much as the victim, but at the time literally can't control it. If you make a big deal of it, she can get stuck in the guilt aspect, which brings a sadness she can't easily move on from and makes going on with her routine difficult at best.

Try to find out if the behavior was meant to communicate a need or frustration. Meet that need if possible. Confirm with the child that the behavior was not an appropriate way to get her needs met, but do not exaggerate verbal discipline. Help the child address her needs (as best you can understand them).

Use whatever means of communication work best with your child, such as symbols, gestures, or language, to help her let you know what was going on when the behavior occurred.

(continues)

FIGURE 1.2 Continued.

Behavior	Potential Response by Parent to Average Child	Potential Response by Parent to Less Impacted Developmentally Disabled Child	Potential Response to Complex Developmentally Disabled Child
Excessive noise or activity in a public setting.	Ask the child to be quiet.	Ask the child to be quiet and/or redirect him.	Recognize your frustration and hers in trying to understand. Attempt to redirect child to some other activity. Generally save your breath in terms of asking him to be quiet. As a general rule, terms like *inside voice* or *be quiet* are lost because he is so out of focus with what is going on or not going on he doesn't even hear you. Observe his behavior in such settings, and be as prepared as possible for avoiding it. Make every attempt to redirect him to some other activity, such as reading him a story in the doctor's waiting room. See chapter 14, "Creating a Community for Your Child," for more ideas on avoidance of behaviors in public.

| Excessive noise at home. | Ask child to be quiet or to go to an area where she can make noise without disrupting others. | Ask the child to use *inside voice*.

Attempt to redirect. Send child to her room or some area where noise can be more tolerated. | Again, save your breath about telling child to be quiet.

Attempt to redirect child to new activity.

Attempt to ascertain why child is being noisy and address that issue rather than the noise.

Maybe she is confused about what comes next in her day. Go over planning either verbally or using whatever communication schedule she uses.

Ascertain if she needs or wants something, using her best communication methods. Attempt to meet those needs.

Evaluate if something might be bothering her such as noise from a fluorescent light or a vacuum cleaner, etc. Reduce noise irritation as much as is feasible. Does she have a pain somewhere, etc.?

If nothing works and you have been unable to redirect her, make sure she is safe and allow her to "get it out of her system." |
| --- | --- | --- | --- |

things better. I am not going to give you technical and specific instructions for any particular diagnosis. What I offer are procedures for figuring out your own child and communicating him to his world by creating a system that works for you at home and in the community. I cannot do that for you, but I hope to help you to do it for your child and for the whole family.

C H A P T E R 2

Billy Ray's Story

BILLY RAY CAME to my late husband, Raymond, and me when he was fifteen months old, with the label of Down syndrome, suffering from malnourishment, and battling chronic ear infections. He had been hospitalized a month before placement for total dehydration resulting from severe ear infections. We were his second adoptive placement, the other lasting only four months. He had been in two foster homes before the failed adoptive placement. Thus we were his fourth home in fifteen short months.

At placement, Billy Ray did not walk and was still on soy formula in a bottle and baby food. We took him to the pediatrician the day after placement. He found that Billy Ray had a resistant strain of ear infection to the medication we were receiving, so he changed the medication. The doctor told me to get him off baby food and on table food. This was

Friday, and we were to bring him back the following Monday for a re-check.

Raymond immediately purchased a blender we could use to chop table food for him and we stocked up on softer foods. Getting Billy Ray to eat was no problem. Keeping him satisfied was the problem. He seemed starved. He had gained three pounds by the time he saw the doctor again on Monday.

Billy Ray seemed to bloom before our eyes, both in improved health and development. He became increasingly active, which we perceived as his eagerness to get on with life. When I cooked dinner, he loved to play in the cupboard with pots and pans or with plastic measuring spoons and cups.

Billy Ray seemed driven to catch up on milestones. He learned to walk on his own. We put him in a walker for only a few days or so it seemed. He was immediately running in it. Soon he was pulling himself up by the bay window where his larger toys were displayed. He would then grab onto his little toy-box wagon and push it all over the family room. Eventually he just let loose and was taking steps on his own.

Someone asked me, in front of the attorney I worked for, if Billy Ray was walking yet. My boss answered, "No, he went right to running" before I could respond. That is an accurate description. Once he started bloom-ing, he hurried through everything.

Potty training worked well initially. Mom said to start him at about eighteen months old. No one told me that Down syndrome children often aren't potty trained until much later, so I just worked with him. He loved his little potty chair. I even have a picture of Billy Ray with his little basketball hoop sitting next to his potty chair. One day, I had put him on the potty chair (which sat in the hall outside the bathroom be-cause our bathroom was too small) and went to answer the telephone. When I came back, I discovered that he had gotten up and brought his basketball hoop from his bedroom. He was sitting there playing basket-ball.

JOY TURNED TO FRUSTRATION

With the snap of a finger (or so it seemed) the pure joy of this sweet little boy turned to frustration. I had known about Down syndrome for years.

My expectations were that Billy Ray would stay sweet, loving, and compliant based on my experience. With his rapid development, he entered the terrible-twos phase even before his second birthday. He was into everything he could get his hands on. Occasionally he would pick up some object and just hurl it at no particular target. It seemed a compulsion on his part that he did not seem able to control.

Just past two years old, Billy Ray developed an ear infection that turned into multiple infections. He ended up in the hospital to get intravenous fluids. While there, he refused to use the toilet even when we brought his little potty chair, and he refused to drink anything. He started being incontinent again, and the doctor put him back on the bottle to get him to take enough liquids when he came home.

Day care and preschool providers complained that he would destroy displays, knock everything off tables, dump every basket of toys. Behavior at home was similar. He had to be watched every minute unless he was asleep. Family and friends felt he was spoiled and undisciplined. I spoke to the pediatrician about it often. However, when we went to her office Billy Ray was calm and smiling. Her experience with him and ours at home were two different things. She assured me that he was just normally active and would get better.

He was going through day care providers at rapid speed because he was so hyperactive and he had so many "accidents" because he no longer responded to potty training. Every time I took him to the doctor, the stimulation of being in her office would calm him down to the cute little boy he used to be, so she could not observe the hyperactivity. She did not seem to believe that he had actually been potty trained. She told me many children with Down syndrome are not trained until five or six years old.

ATTENTION DEFICIT HYPERACTIVITY DISORDER

By the time he was five years old, Billy Ray was about to be kicked out of Head Start and our marriage was in shambles. When I took him to the developmental pediatrician again, he showed his difficult behavior for the first time. He was dumping containers with tongue depressors, etc. all over the floor and destroying the examining room despite the efforts of the doctor, her nurse, and me. He left with the diagnosis of attention deficit hyperactivity disorder (ADHD) and his first prescription for stimulants.

Having the ADHD label (diagnosis) was a liberating experience in that it proved there was a reason for his behavior other than poor parenting. However, the frustration did not go away. There were medications to deal with and we had to learn about an unfamiliar condition. The pediatrician's frustration began at that point. The stimulants worked great for about two weeks. His metabolism would then adjust to the dose and it would last only about two hours. We needed to adjust the dosage constantly.

When he reached the top of the recommended dose for the stimulants, his pediatrician sent him to a pediatric neurologist. He found nothing other than the ADHD and Down syndrome. He prescribed a drug commonly used for Parkinson's disease, which he thought would help. It did not work and brought potentially serious side effects. Withdrawing the drug was difficult as well. It took the psychiatrist we later saw a year to wean Billy Ray off the medication, because Billy Ray experienced severe withdrawal symptoms every time we tried.

BIPOLAR DISORDER

At age seven, Billy Ray's behavior became totally bizarre. It would sometimes take three people to keep him from doing things that would hurt him, such as trying to put objects into the wood stove or climbing up on bookshelves. Our wonderful pediatrician, who had tried everything she could, said she was in over her head. She referred him to a pediatric psychiatrist.

The psychiatrist, Dr. Ron Roy ("Dr. Ron"), explored several possibilities in an attempt to diagnose and treat Billy Ray. He had me call Billy Ray's adoption worker to see if the adoption agency was aware of any family history of bipolar disorder. No information was available. He said that the best way to diagnose bipolar disorder was family history, but because were unable to do so we had to look at the symptoms.

Dr. Ron believed that bipolar symptoms had manifested earlier than would be expected because we had a family crisis triggered by my husband's car accident and multiple extended hospitalizations. In addition to Daddy being sick, the little pickup that had been special for father and son had been totaled. Billy Ray was not able to understand the difference between the truck and a person. He grieved for it like the loss of a person.

Eventually Dr. Ron was able to stabilize Billy Ray on medication. There were medication adjustments to be made because of his metabolism, and his blood levels always had to be closely monitored. In fact, Billy Ray handled the death of his father (Billy Ray was twelve years at that time) without major mania or difficulty. Unfortunately, the same year my husband died, Dr. Ron died too.

AUTISM

At fourteen years old Billy Ray experienced several major seizures believed to be caused by a medication for ADHD. He was rushed to the hospital by ambulance. The boy I put on the school bus that morning was gone forever. The boy I brought home from the hospital looked like Billy Ray, but he was totally different. Six months after the seizures, when the pediatrician said he should be returning to what was normal for him, Billy Ray was displaying more and more symptoms of autism. Now in his early twenties, his symptoms are comparable to someone with severe autistic symptoms.

It took a couple of frustrating years to realize that Billy Ray could no longer understand "no" or "I don't know" as an answer to requests or questions. If I say no to something he wants, he is not able to understand why. He is not able to put himself into my situation and see that I am busy, that something needs to occur first, or that his request is inappropriate. He will cry, which is abnormal for him, out of frustration because he literally cannot understand my response. This cry is not that of an angry or spoiled child but rather a sad or hurt child. He says, "I try," meaning he wants to try to do or get whatever he requests. It broke my heart when I realized he is not able to accept what to me was a logical and reasonable response. He only knows that I have not met his needs and doesn't understand why I don't always do so.

ADAPTING TO BILLY RAY

The concept of "I said no and that's all there is to it" is not going to work with complex children like Billy Ray. Does that mean you have to give them everything they want? I do not think so. It does mean you must be cautious about how you handle saying no, in order to avoid power struggles and, if this is a problem for your child, aggressive incidents. The best plan is to anticipate a behavior or demand *before* you get into that situation.

For example, I know that if we go into a grocery store or clothing store, he is going to demand more than I am prepared to purchase. Preparation *sometimes* helps alleviate a lot of it. When I know that we are going into a store that is likely to cause trouble, we make a list of things we are going to buy and I reaffirm several times before we go into the store that we will buy only what is on the list. I allow him to add something I can live with to the list, and I make sure he understands that is all he can add. When we pull into the parking lot of the store, I pull out the list, we go over the list, and I ask him if he understands that the items on the list are all we are going to buy. Generally, he accepts that at least in the car. Other times he demands something else. I leave the master lock set on the car doors and we delay going into the store. Depending on his level of insistence, the urgency for the shopping, help I might or might not have at home, we might just go for a ride and then come back and try again, or we might go home. Sometimes the process of driving away is enough to correct the problem, and he will agree because he wants what he put on the list.

Preparation does not always work. In those cases when he demands something else, I decide whether his demand is so inappropriate that I have to get into a power struggle in public. For us that can mean he throws himself on the floor and does not get up for extended periods of time, people walk around him and stare at me and at him, and the manager and sometimes the security guard come by. Instead of saying no at the start, I say, "look on the list" and point out that the item is not there.

Billy Ray and I were in a grocery one time with one of his caregivers. This particular store created many problems for us in that twelve-packs of soda were at the end of almost every aisle (we were having a heat wave that summer). The doctor had asked us to limit Billy Ray to a minimum of soda at the time. Limiting it if we have it in the house is not workable. The caregiver attempted to block him and he scratched her trying to push her out of the way. He lay down on the floor and would not give up for what seemed an eternity (probably ten minutes). People were walking over him and the manager had made several trips to check on us. At some point, you have to conclude the situation. Unless your child is small enough that you can just pick her up, you have to negotiate. I offered him one can of pop but not the whole twelve pack. The caregiver pointed out that I had let him win. That is only partially true. I felt it was a win-win situation. He did not bring the twelve-pack home where I knew he would have consumed it too quickly. He felt he won in that he got one soda.

GOING OUT IN PUBLIC

When he was little and functioned on a higher level, Billy Ray got used to going everywhere with me, including many of my professional commitments. Because of my work demands and the frequency of my late husband's hospitalizations, we ate in restaurants a lot of the time. He thrived on community contact. Because I also thrive on being out in public, staying home with him would be punishment to both of us. We both need to get out in the world.

Billy Ray is not satisfied with fast-food drive-through windows. He wants "restaurant." As much as he wants to go, it is stressful for him, especially if the service is slow. If he has to wait long, he can be noisy. For this purpose, I want to address the question of why it is worth the effort to get out.

Agreeing to "lunch—restaurant" helps greatly to get Billy Ray's compliance with medical appointments or going to the lab for a blood test. Additionally, given our country location and the distance we travel to most of our medical contacts, it is usually necessary to dine out for at least one meal. Because these trips are more stressful, he is more likely to demonstrate negative behaviors or agitation during lunch. During a particularly difficult episode, he was noisy and people were actually moving to tables farther away from us. The caregiving assistant said she thought we should not take Billy Ray into restaurants anymore because the other customers were paying for their meals too and they had a right to enjoy them.

I was livid to think that this caregiver would suggest that Billy Ray should be permanently isolated. I have repeatedly seen how withdrawn or even angry Billy Ray gets when he does not get out of the house regularly. However, the logic of the caregiver's observation hit home. It would certainly be easier for the other customers, the staff, myself, and even for Billy Ray to keep him home. However, he needs the illogical in this case too. It meant coming up with as many solutions as possible to make it easier and to create a comfortable community for him.

Certainly staying home or bringing home hamburgers or pizza (which Billy Ray wouldn't likely eat anyway) would be easier than trying to minimize his disruptive behavior and deal with public scrutiny of it. Neither Billy Ray nor I would be happy with that much isolation. We both need the contact that comes from a community. Difficult as it is to accomplish, it revitalizes us both.

A WORD ABOUT "SPECIAL NEEDS"

In order to classify the extra needs of people who experience disabilities, society has come up with the term *special needs*. This brings with it many connotations that are not always clear. The word *special* is often used to describe something wonderful. Growing up, I can remember being told we were going to get a "special treat." Listening to someone talk about a "special-needs child," you might think that child is an angel who is loving all the time. When he behaves differently than expected, he drops off that pedestal quickly. I think the term *extraordinary needs* would be better. Billy Ray does have more needs than are ordinary, but that does not make him special. He is special because of who he is, not because of his needs.

C H A P T E R

3

NOT YET THE BEST OF TIMES

LIKE THE OPENING LINES of Charles Dickens's A Tale of Two Cities, the world you and your disabled child live in could be described as "the best of times" and "the worst of times." More is known about developmental disabilities than at any other time in history, but there is still much to discover. Laws such as the Americans with Disabilities Act (the ADA) and the Individuals with Disabilities Education Act (IDEA) provide many services never dreamed of fifty years ago. At the same time, new cases of autism alone are occurring in epidemic proportions. Other disabilities are on the rise as well. Existing educational and other services are having difficulty keeping up.

In reality, some of the changes have created confusion and conflict on many fronts. Professionals and parents often are pitted against each other; professionals will even turn against other professionals in what can become big disputes. Eligibility for assistance and special education requires demonstrated need for special services. Beyond that, however, it is also necessary to prove that your child can benefit from the services, not just that he or she is eligible. The red tape in trying to prove a child's need for specific services tangles easily.

A common brag in the developmental disabilities community is that we are so far from the level of care provided in the 1950s, when most children were placed in institutions. The pressure to place complex children in facilities still exists. Facilities are not the same as the big institutions. Some do a great job at meeting the needs of the population they serve. Others appear motivated by business factors. Children with specific complexities may not fit the criteria for a facility in their area. Suggested placements may be several states away from the family home.

A DIAGNOSIS MERRY-GO-ROUND

Diagnosis strongly affects a child's eligibility for services, educational programs, and treatment. Expectations of a child's abilities and predictions for his future are determined based on diagnoses. Sometimes coming up with a firm diagnosis is complicated. Children may perform or behave one way in the doctor's office or at school and quite another way when in a more comfortable setting. Your child's problems may be too complicated to explain in a short visit with the doctor or educational professional.

As parents, especially first-time parents, we may not know what information is important to share with the professional. My first husband and I decided to adopt a child with Down syndrome because of my years of experience working with children and adults with this condition. When Billy Ray's activity level at home and school was difficult to control at age three, we related that to the pediatrician, who felt his activity was normal. The stimulation of visiting her office consistently calmed him sufficiently to affect his behavior. Two years later, at the age of five, when he trashed her examining room despite the doctor, her nurse, and myself trying to stop him, a diagnosis of ADHD was finally made.

I did not recognize any symptoms of autism at that time. A diagnosis of autism generally is made by three years old. Billy Ray did not demonstrate specific symptoms of autism until age fourteen—following the medication reaction that caused his series of seizures. There was much disagreement about the diagnosis because most of the symptoms were so delayed. However, when I finally pushed for an autism evaluation, the autism specialist showed me where Billy Ray had minor symptoms even as a young child. For example, he loved to watch fireworks on television but the noise from actually attending a fireworks display terrorized him. He preferred to play by himself rather than with other children. His favorite play was lining up his toys in a row rather than playing with them as toys. Some clothes seemed to irritate him and he scratched constantly. Without knowing the possible significance of those and other signs, I never told the developmental pediatrician about any of them, except the scratching.

Children are categorized into little boxes generally corresponding to their diagnoses. It is easier for society to fit our children into existing systems. If a child has one diagnosis or level of intelligence, he is expected to function a certain way. He cannot be expected to achieve beyond a certain point. Children like your child "usually" experience things one way or another depending on their diagnoses. *Wrong!* Your child is an individual. He needs to have his life adapted to however he can function best, no matter what the diagnosis says is "usual."

Some children do not fit into little boxes. Down syndrome children are expected to be quiet and sweet like we see portrayed on television. Autistic children are commonly believed to be unable to make eye contact or form social relationships. However, children may form relationships although they have more severe problems associated with autism. There are children who experience both autism and Down syndrome, so that symptoms do not manifest themselves in the stereotypes for either condition. We are learning about connections between ADHD, autism, and other disabilities as time goes on. Other combinations of diagnoses, such as developmental disabilities and mental-illness diagnoses, make treatment options more difficult to find. Sometimes there are no clear-cut diagnoses for a child. All of these children and others who do not respond to traditional programs or treatments need individual solutions adapted to their understanding, abilities, and needs.

Billy Ray was stuck in what we called the diagnosis merry-go-round for many years. Depending upon whom you talk with, he experiences Down syndrome, bipolar disorder, ADHD, and autism. Trying to treat the combination is a course in frustration for professionals as well as parents.

ADVOCATING FOR YOUR CHILD

When a child's needs or abilities are unclear, he is often pushed into programs that do not work for him. Maybe the only way he has to communicate that it is not working is through agitation, property destruction, or even aggression. Substantiating the needs or strengths of your developmentally disabled child in order to get appropriate services and education for him is not a slam dunk. Adequate funding does not always come with the legislation mandating services. Educators and agencies are not willing to put out funds from overly strapped budgets unless they are sure of the need for the services. It takes good advocacy skills, especially if the child does not clearly demonstrate the ability to benefit from the desired services.

Numerous parents have e-mailed my Parenting Your Complex Child website (www.parentingyourcomplexchild.com) bragging about how strong they are in advocating for their children. A recurrent statement is that they "kick butt"—meaning they fight hard for their children. But true advocating is team building for the mutual good of a disabled child or adult. Fighting among the parent and the professionals generally slows or stops the progress. The victim is the child. Parents may "win" a battle here and there but lose the war in the end. More can be accomplished if the educational or other team members work together with parents. I'll talk about working toward that goal in chapter 13.

Having read several books written by Temple Grandin, Ph.D., about her own experiences with having autism, I was excited when I saw that her mother, Eustacia Cutler, had written A Thorn in My Pocket (Future Horizons, 2004), about raising Dr. Grandin. I knew from Dr. Grandin's own books that she had been diagnosed with autism in 1950. I expected to see huge differences in services between then and now. Reading it, I chuckled at how many things we still have to negotiate—just as Mrs. Cutler did in the 1950s—to get help for our children today.

Mrs. Cutler worked with private schools for the most part. There are more services available through public programs today, but we must demonstrate a child's need for specific services and his ability to benefit (for example, the ability to stay focused long enough to participate) from those services. Parents with children whose problems are as complicated as my son's still experience the frustration Mrs. Cutler described in finding appropriate education and assistance for her daughter.

I have experienced pressure from family and professionals to place my son out of the home just as Mrs. Cutler experienced. She used her creativity to make a life for Temple, because she found the alternatives undesirable and wanted more for her daughter. Parents still need to do that today. I create community activities based on what I know my son's interests and strengths are, just as Mrs. Cutler recognized Temple's abilities and interest in sewing and arranged a summer job with a local tailor.

What Mrs. Cutler did is still necessary for our complex children today. She became an advocate and guide for her daughter. Dr. Grandin has used her autism to achieve incredible success. In many of her books, Dr. Grandin credits her mother for playing a major role in her success.

It is not my intention to retell Temple Grandin's story. She has done that herself in *Emergence: Labeled Autistic* (Temple Grandin, Ph.D., and Margaret M. Scariano, Warner Books, 1996), as well as in many of her other books. Her mother shares the story in *A Thorn in My Pocket* referenced above. However, lest you think your child is more difficult for you than Temple Grandin was to her mother, here is a passage from *A Thorn in My Pocket* about behavior Temple exhibited as a child:

> "Temple rips off her lilac flowered wallpaper in long jagged shreds, digs through her blue plastic crib mattress with its bunny rabbits, claws between the springs, pulls out the stuffing. Flings it about, eats it, chews it, spits it in great gray wads. She goes into a spasm of giggling and spitting. I try to calm her, she scratches free and runs out the front door. In the middle of the road, our country road with the stone wall running along it, she yanks off her clothes, squats and poops. Again I try to scoop her up. She laughs her crazy laugh and squirms from my arms."

Mrs. Cutler's reaction to the situation was "I repaper her room and fight despair." If she had given up and placed Temple in an institution instead of guiding her, the world might have lost a valuable asset in helping us understand autism from the inside out. Her mother's creativity in finding the right resources and advocating for Dr. Grandin helped her to succeed in life. Today if a child demonstrates similar behavior, she might be diagnosed with one or more behavior disorders. She might be heavily medicated or placed in some form of out-of-home placement. I cringe to think how many more Temple Grandins are lost in their own worlds and fail to achieve their full potential because their parents feel so defeated in trying to help their children find the way.

As a result of Dr. Grandin's ability to communicate her experiences with autism, professionals and parents understand the condition as never before. She has been referred to as a treasure in the field of autism. Mrs. Cutler's role was important in developing this treasure as well. Who knows what treasure you are developing in your child?

Temple Grandin's success despite her struggle with autism is certainly above average. The degree of functioning or intelligence is not what matters. Every child has something to offer his world. The goal is to help him be the best that he can be. Mrs. Cutler used her own creativity to help Temple find her own path. You can change the life of your child too.

YOUR CHILD IN THE REAL WORLD

Dr. Ron, Billy Ray's pediatric psychiatrist, in a sense has been a mentor to me from his grave. Dr. Ron used to explain that medical schools cannot possibly anticipate every set of circumstances, especially with the combination of diagnoses that may make symptoms manifest differently in individual children. Given the rapid change in what we know and the rise in the number of special-needs children, this is likely even truer today.

Changes in the real world you and your child live in may not have caught up with the progress anticipated by legislation such as the ADA and IDEA. Equal access to a sometimes-hostile environment is not always progress. Businesses must accommodate the special needs of your child. No legislation can reduce rudeness, insensitivity, and fear by other patrons. Disabled persons and their family/caregivers experience hostility and intolerance in many ways. Parents may get the message subtly or even directly that that they should keep their children away from the public.

I became acquainted with the manager of a restaurant in our former community. That community was near a large institution that closed. The residents were incorporated into the community. Some moved to foster and group homes, and others returned to their family homes in that community. Though we regularly visited the restaurant, we never saw any other developmentally disabled children there. This surprised me because this restaurant goes the extra mile to make everything nice for Billy Ray. I asked the manager if we were just there at the wrong times to see other disabled customers.

The restaurant manager explained that other customers often mistreated the families of disabled children. She said many times these families would just leave without even eating or finishing their meals and not return following these experiences.

In chapter 14, I'll talk about how to work with the community resources that your child visits most often in order to create a comfortable environment for him and for others he will encounter in those settings.

LEARNING FROM YOUR CHILD

Parents' expertise and understanding of their individual children are just as necessary in 2006 as they were in 1950 when Mrs. Cutler was trying to encourage and guide her daughter, Temple. The success of your child is greatly affected by you, her parent, taking your rightful place as leader of her team.

What I will share in chapters 4 through 16 might be called "bootstrap learning"—lessons I was forced to absorb as I tried to help Billy Ray. I grew tired of hearing "you are doing the best you can" from doctors and educators. I took him to specialist after specialist. Several medications were tried that either did not work or caused difficult side effects. He was frequently called "one of the most complicated patients I have ever worked with." Eventually it became clear that part of the problem was that the professionals were having difficulty seeing Billy Ray as he really is. However, the journals I kept were far too long to share with a busy professional. Creating a more concise format that could be conveyed during short appointments made treatment and program recommendations much more likely to work.

The methods contained in this book, including the documentation system in chapter 12, are intended to help parents understand their own child even better. You will learn how to adapt circumstances as needed to make things easier for the family unit as a whole, and you will learn how to advocate in such a way that the professionals see your child as he really is. My suggestions are based on a child's natural responses to daily life rather than his diagnosis.

Going with the flow and doing whatever the professionals recommend may seem easier than the work involved in following these suggestions. But keep in mind that medication and program trials that may not work may frustrate you and your child. In addition to the side effects of medications, treatment, or programs, these things may also affect your child's behavior and general functioning. Making his home or community more comfortable for him and communicating his needs and abilities to those involved in his life save a good deal of that frustration.

One thing that hasn't changed over the years is the need for parents to encourage and support their children to the degree necessary in finding the path for them. In *Emergence: Labeled Autistic*, Dr. Grandin shares her struggle to find her way. She says her mother told her, "Every person needs to find her door and open it. No one can do it for her." Not everyone could explain as eloquently as Dr. Grandin what door is right for her. But given the time and patience, children can communicate who they are and what they can do by their individual responses to specific situations, if not by verbal communication. They can find their door, but they need more help in finding it than other children.

As parents, we need to advocate for research that will teach us more about disabilities and better treatment options, and legislation that will help provide better services and benefits. At the same time, we need to be advocates for our own children to ensure they get the individualized services they need right now. Your child and mine need meaningful lives, whatever that means to them. They cannot wait for more knowledge and better laws. Those things might come too slowly.

4

Feeling Misunderstood

I HAVE SPENT A LOT OF TIME thinking about you, the reader, and about your child. I imagined sitting with you on my deck looking at Mt. Hood or the fog that might be blocking it. I would share the successes and failures along my journey as Billy Ray's mom. Mostly I would listen to you vent, because that is probably your least-met need. The pat answers given to parents would only leave you frustrated, so I would avoid those. There would be comic relief sharing stories of how we have felt misunderstood by even those we expected to understand and the cute things our kids had done. Above all else, you and I would both feel some familiarity with each other's situation. We would be kindred spirits— which are not so easy to find when you are raising a complex child.

Parenting any child is challenging. When some difficulty such as an illness or disability is present, it is even more so. When you have a complex child who tends to challenge even the medical and educational professionals, solutions involve more than technical procedures and professional advice. They also involve patience, endurance, frustration, and much self-control. The irony is that often your child may cause you less frustration than those involved in his care and education. Much of the time it feels like no one really understands, including the people you expect to be the most understanding: professionals and your closest family and friends. The sense of isolation from the rest of the world, including sometimes your spouse, can be lonely and painful.

You may feel judged by people you know have no clue what a struggle your day-to-day life is. If your child wears dirty clothes to school or the doctor and is not freshly bathed, it appears that you do not take proper care of your child. In reality, it may be that your child refuses to change clothes or bathe. If he behaves inappropriately, he may appear undisciplined when in reality he is confused. If you do not correct him, you may be accused of spoiling him. Often when you take your child out of his environment, even to the doctor, he will behave entirely differently than at home. Billy Ray often behaves better in public than at home because he is frightened. That makes it even more difficult to gain understanding from others. Surprisingly, even parents of other disabled children may not be able to identify with your situation.

You may go through life feeling exhausted, sad, frustrated, or angry. If you are angry with school or medical personnel, people just assume you are grieving or in denial regarding your child's disability. Certainly, parents do experience grief and denial that might manifest itself in angry outbursts at meetings. However, frustration at trying to be heard or get appropriate services for your child may be the cause of angry outbursts as well.

Instead of feeling good when someone says, "I wish other parents cared for their children the way you do," it makes me sad and even angry. I do not believe that I care about Billy Ray more. It is my belief that the very systems set up to help our kids often defeat the parents. Nevertheless, if parents do not come to planning meetings or follow up on appointments, they may be accused of not caring.

LEFT OUT IN THE COLD

I will deal with this point more fully in chapter 13. For purposes of this chapter, I would like to give you just one example of how the system often defeats the parents. I had been working with the autism specialist to create a more workable school schedule for Billy Ray, because school was not working out well for him. The specialist visited with folks in the school building to research projects that might be available for Billy Ray to do, similar to those Billy Ray had done in his most successful year. The specialist created some communication cues and other materials to help Billy Ray understand tasks better. I was pleased with the ideas created and anxious to share them with the Individual Education Plan (IEP) team at the scheduled meeting. I was sure it would make things better for my son.

I walked into the meeting to find that the entire team including the county case manager had convened a half-hour early for something they called a "premeeting" (a meeting held to plan the meeting before the parents arrive). The autism specialist had presented the plan to school personnel outside of my presence and the school personnel had decided that they could not provide that much structure in their program. The decision to remove Billy Ray from the program was made before I walked through the door. My vote in the matter was of no impact by the time I arrived. There was nothing the autism specialist or I could do at that point.

Given the sense of futility in situations like that, combined with the difficulty of supporting your child(ren) and the struggle to get time off to attend all the meetings, it is obvious why some parents just stop attending those meetings. It has nothing to do with whether they care about their children.

Some people like to say that parents of disabled children are "saints" and that we will have "many jewels in our crown in Heaven." Trust me—I am not a saint. I get impatient with my son and my husband just like every other parent and wife. You probably do too. I get frustrated and even mad at professionals and others if my son is not being treated fairly. I do think loving our children and dealing with their problems, combined with the frustrations of trying to get appropriate help, does help us grow more patient and tolerant.

UNDERSTANDING IS NOT EASY TO FIND

Maybe you have gone to support groups to try to get some insight and encouragement. You may be able to identify with other parents and find a great deal of support even if your children have only one label or two that are commonly together. If your child has symptoms of several conditions or syndromes, chances are he doesn't manifest classic symptoms of anything. In that case, it is very difficult for you to explain your child to the group or for the group to offer the help it tries hard to provide. This is especially true if your child has a developmental-delay diagnosis *and* a mental-illness diagnosis. The waters get so murky, it is difficult to get support.

Wanting to be understood is a natural desire both for you and your child. Billy Ray becomes more agitated and aggressive when he is unable to communicate something he needs or wants. It is likely the same with you, except you don't show the aggression that your child does. You want your friends to understand. Realistically it is very difficult for some folks to relate to your life or your child. That does not mean you should throw away all your friends. Close friends will generally make an effort to relate to you and your child. It will take energy on both sides but can be very rewarding for your child as well as for you. Friends who are more casual sort of disappear, partially because they do not know how to relate. That can make you feel like you and your child have been rejected.

Eventually I found that it was worth putting my energy into maintaining a smaller circle of friends than to continue to try to maintain the larger circle I had before Billy Ray's situation became complex. Close friends will learn to overlook shortcomings in you and your child. It becomes more comfortable to have even one friend who listens and tries to understand than to be repeatedly trying to explain why your child just threw a trinket or spilled his milk.

Perhaps the most painful experience is when your closest friends and family are not able to understand. They might see negative behaviors or aggression toward you but cannot put themselves in your or your child's position. You may know that your child throws himself on the floor or strikes out at you because he is frustrated at trying to communicate his needs, his wishes, or his confusion about what is happening to him at that moment. Unless someone is around him a lot, your child may appear to others as a naughty child who is being spoiled by his parent.

Your family has sort of a double-bind situation. They may love your child, but they also love you and see the difficulty, even in part, that you go through. They wonder why you keep your child at home instead of in some other appropriate placement. It has been my observation that those appropriate placements are suggested for the benefit of the family, and they are not always the best places for the child.

Recently we traveled to another part of the state and visited the home of an uncle with whom I had been very close as a young child. He is great with children and a loving man. Billy Ray refused to get out of the car, which was abnormal for him. Because I didn't know why Billy Ray was doing this, I left him in the car with my husband, Larry. Uncle Don was open about his concern that I had sacrificed so much of my life. He pointed out that I could not even relax and enjoy visiting him because I had to worry about my son and my husband outside in the car. He was not badmouthing my son, but he said, "You are my niece and I worry about you too." That hurt for several days. After much thought I realized that it is impossible for people to understand the commitment you feel and the choice you make regarding your child. The choice to keep a complex child at home is not a choice everyone would make. It is a very personal decision and difficult for others to grasp.

PUBLIC AWARENESS IS A MIXED BAG

The media presents many pictures of "special children." Most are high functioning, like Corky, a character in the long-running television series *Life Goes On.* Corky experienced Down syndrome but was able to communicate well and achieve many things. Someone like Corky is probably more the exception than the average child who experiences Down syndrome.

Media attention has brought some acceptance to developmentally disabled children. Unfortunately, children and adults who show some of the physical characteristics of more commonly known conditions such as Down syndrome are expected to be quiet and pleasant. When such a child begins to demonstrate behaviors that don't fit with the stereotypes, tolerance and acceptance may evaporate rather quickly.

Although understanding for developmentally disabled children and adults in general is improving, understanding for the more complex kids and their parents is not progressing to the same degree. Because these kids can frighten or, at the very least, disturb others with their noise and rapid movements, there is not the same tolerance or social acceptance. The desire that complex children who have behavior issues should be kept at home or in a facility out of view of the public is often communicated subtly—or even not so subtly—to the parents.

You may pick up books that appear to have many answers for your child but little comparison to your child. Procedural and technical help from these books is nice, but unless you can see some comparison to your child, they don't help much. I recently bought a book that I thought was going to be helpful. The author had expertise and was a parent of a disabled child. However, I was disappointed to read that the author wondered what people must think when they see him and his child. He didn't mention how public scrutiny must feel to his child, nor did he give insight into his own feelings as a parent.

As I stated earlier, Billy Ray has been two types of child. He was charming and socially confident as a younger child. Now, as a young adult with more complex problems, he is not always socially acceptable. When he came to us as a toddler with a diagnosis of Down syndrome, he was the personification of cute and sweet. At age twenty-three, he still can be sweet and attractive in public. But more often he is noisy and bouncing, speaks profanity that he doesn't understand (so he uses it inappropriately), occasionally throws objects and/or will throw himself on the floor, or will refuse to leave a public place. When we went to restaurants and stores before his medication reaction, people would stare, partially because he has special needs, but mostly because he was just so cute and funny. People would give up their places in line for a table if they saw the table next to us was about to leave. The hosts would say things like, "Everyone wants to sit by Billy Ray tonight." Since his personality change, people stare with annoyance and irritation, sometimes make rude comments, and may move to another table away from us.

THE STRUGGLE FOR ACCEPTANCE

It is very difficult for other people to understand that your child may not be able to be disciplined or reasoned with. Before the medication reaction, you could reason with Billy Ray easily. He understood when he needed to be patient or if I was saying "no" to him. After he changed, I would say "no" for some reason and he would not let it drop. I have come to realize that he is so focused on whatever his need or request is that he is no longer able to just let things go. Family, friends, and the public can observe illogical requests from him or accommodations that I make as spoiling him.

Continuing to struggle for understanding and acceptance of you and your child may prolong your frustration. One of the first things I dealt with in trying to pick myself up by the bootstraps and start again was prioritizing what was important in the grand scheme of life's journey. Our whole lifestyle had to be reevaluated when Billy Ray changed. Rethinking how important it is or isn't to have everyone understand can be freeing.

I needed to accept that:

- People do not always understand what day-to-day life involves for your child and for you. This means recognizing that because children often behave differently out of the security of home, it is impossible for most folks to understand.

- I must decide how important it is for someone to understand and then prioritize the energy I will put into communicating to that person. If you meet a rude person in a store or restaurant, you might decide it is not worth it and ignore that person. If the person is a medical or special-education professional, put all the energy you can into determining the best method of communicating your child to them. That way, suggestions and decisions the professional makes regarding your child's care will be informed decisions.

- Even with professionals, I would have to try someone else if I have put a realistic effort into communicating Billy Ray to them and they can't or won't understand. You are your child's most important advocate, so allow yourself to find a new professional, if necessary, who can relate to your child and to you.

TAKE CARE OF YOURSELF TOO

I have removed this section from my manuscript several times because I know how much I balked at this advice over the years. We hate to hear that we have to take care of ourselves so we can take care of our children. Putting it into practice is hard even if we accept it in principle. The advice of Billy Ray's longtime developmental pediatrician, Dr. Mary Lynn O'Brien, was always to take care of myself too. Looking back, it is clear that it is the only advice consistently not taken.

Sometimes the person you may need the most understanding from is yourself. It is hard to allow yourself to be human. When your child is constantly illogical, extremely noisy, aggressive, and/or asking the same questions repeatedly, you may lose your patience from time to time. Generally, this can be as devastating to you as it is to your child. You just get tired of being punched or having your child scream in your ears. You expect yourself to have superior strength to accept what is intolerable to many people. Give yourself the same patience and understanding you work so hard to give your child.

When you do lose your patience, make peace quickly with your child. Tell her you are sorry that you were impatient, that you will try to be more understanding and patient in the future. Then give yourself a break. Recognize that if you are losing your cool, you need to get away from your child, even for just a few minutes. If possible, get someone to watch her for a short time and get out of the house. If you cannot get relief care, see if you can find an activity for your child such as watching a favorite movie or even taking a nap. Then treat yourself to a bubble bath, do your nails, or read a book just for you that's not about her needs. Even if she is an escape risk, you can do something for yourself while in the same room with her. Put a chair in the doorway to her room, sit down and read a book, or put your favorite CD in a personal CD player.

You want to help your child succeed. But whether it is taking care of your family, advocating for your child in school, meeting with medical personnel, or experimenting with the ideas that follow, you can do only so much. Do what you can without pushing yourself beyond your strength. If you are stressed, your child will be too. Slow progress is better for both of you.

Getting care for your child so you can go to your own medical and dental appointments is difficult, let alone finding time to go to the gym or do something else for yourself. Clothing, haircuts, and other things that you need for your own self-esteem often can take last place. They tap overly strained budgets and energy. They seem like things you can skip. Then it catches up with you. One day you look in the mirror and wonder how you got to this point.

Personal care is a common area of misunderstanding. If you struggle to get your child ready for an event or appointment, he may be in much better condition when you arrive than you are. This was really brought home to me recently when I spoke to someone about appropriate attire for me when speaking to parent groups.

In trying to explain to my friend, who is so skilled at looking nice, I realized there was no way she could possibly understand. Unless you live it, you cannot know what it is like to fight with your child to get him ready for an outing, not sure you are going to make it at all. If your child finally cooperates, you can get him to church in his Sunday best while you have thrown jeans on and brushed your hair wet because there is no time left to dry and curl it. You either have to go that way or stay home.

I now can see that the times I have taken the best care of myself have been times that Billy Ray has done better too. Looking over old journals, I realized that when I began to pull myself out of the rut of self-neglect, things got better for my son as well. Whether it is that as a parent there was more to give when refilling my own "bucket" or that he was doing better so I had more energy for myself is not always clear. Our complex children notice what we are feeling. They may not understand why we are feeling down, but they know something is wrong. As we feel better about ourselves, it has a strong impact on how they feel too.

WORKING WITH DOCTORS

THE RELATIONSHIP BETWEEN you and your child's doctors is vital. The most cordial of relationships can have unrealistic expectations and misunderstandings on both sides. It is important to remember that doctors are people first. As in any field, there are caring, conscientious professionals, and there are those who have their own agendas. Some doctors will communicate better than other doctors. Education and experience does not free them of all human traits and weaknesses. Frustrations and problems occur for them just as for you. A natural emotional bond may develop when a doctor has been caring for the same patient repeatedly for a long time. They experience sadness when their patients have crises or do not respond to their best attempts at treatment.

Society expects doctors to have all the answers and solutions to any problem that comes along. Whether they see themselves as almost god-like or not, there is a tendency to put doctors on that level of respect.

This makes it hard for some parents to stand up and make doctors listen to their concerns, and it is even harder for some doctors to admit they do not have the answers. As parents, we feel a strong need to rely on doctors' opinions and to follow their recommendations to the letter. We may even think the doctor can somehow "fix" our child.

The difficulty in relating to doctors is further complicated by their schedules. Many doctors leave private practices, where they are able to control their schedules a bit more, because the cost makes surviving outside of a health maintenance organization (HMO) difficult. Some HMOs schedule as many as six patients in an hour. That's only ten minutes per person while the doctor must also handle other routine tasks such as returning telephone calls during that hour.

WANTED: MORE SPECIALISTS

Developmental pediatricians are skilled at treating developmental disabilities and medical issues. Making psychiatric diagnoses for patients with developmental delays may take them out of their comfort zones. For psychiatrists without that added specialty, dealing with a child who is developmentally delayed can make diagnosing mental-health issues—let alone treating them—complicated. Although more psychiatrists are specializing in the mental-health issues of the developmentally disabled, there are still too few to meet the needs of that increasing population. That specialty requires an exceptional commitment on the doctor's part, because many patients have no insurance other than Medicaid, Medicare, and various state health plans that pay considerably less for services than many private plans.

According to the National Association for the Dually Diagnosed (an association for people with both developmental disabilities and mental-illness diagnoses), a survey of doctors in the state of Illinois found that, out of 312 respondents (a 24 percent response rate), 95 percent acknowledged that they treat patients with developmental disabilities and 70 percent acknowledged that they had no formal training in the area. The results in most other states would probably be no better, if not actually worse.

When our first pediatric psychiatrist retired due to illness, we were moved around to several psychiatrists because his replacement was slow to join our HMO. I remember asking several of the psychiatrists who saw Billy Ray in the interim if they were experienced with developmental disabilities. The pat answer seemed to be, "We all do a few cases." That was not a comforting answer, given my son's complexity.

DIFFICULTIES IN DIAGNOSING COMPLEX CHILDREN

If a professional can find a label (diagnosis), treatment may be more obvious and things are clearer. This can provide security for both parents and professionals. When we know what we are dealing with, we are more comfortable. The very structure of how we get services pressures professionals to find labels. Eligibility for many governmental or educational services, as well as health-plan policies, is based upon diagnosis. In the real world, some children and adults do not fit clear-cut diagnoses.

Not all diagnoses have straightforward tests to verify the diagnosis. Evaluation and diagnosis in such cases must be done based on symptoms. Most complex children are not able to communicate what they experience to the doctor, adding to the complications of diagnosis. The doctor must evaluate based on reports from the parents or caregivers. This becomes complicated for busy professionals who have little time to spend with patients. Parents are anxious to get all the information to the doctor in rapid speed, given the limited time. Out of that frustration, parents may talk quickly and speak in fragments that prevent the doctor from clearly understanding what is being communicated. Mistakes in diagnosis or treatment can occur if the doctor is not able to get a realistic picture of the child's functioning or symptoms. Parents may give the doctor far too many details to absorb but leave out the very detail that would affect diagnosis or treatment, because they don't realize its importance.

BILLY RAY'S DOCTORS

The fact that Billy Ray has not remained consistently stable is no reflection on the doctors he has had over the years. Billy Ray is blessed to be twenty-three years old and to have had only three pediatricians since his placement with us at fifteen months old. The first and second (both developmental pediatricians) shared him for a few months, and then one of them moved to another clinic within our HMO but remained available when our regular pediatrician wasn't. The one who remained at our clinic, Dr. Mary Lynn O'Brien, took care of him from the time he was about seventeen months old until he was nineteen years old, when she retired. Her practice has been taken over by Dr. Edward Ruden, a very kind man who loves my son, and we work well together. Still, we miss Dr. O'Brien as the family member she became in all those years.

We have had numerous psychiatrists, some better than others. I still grieve for Dr. Ron because he taught me so much and I still have so many questions to ask him. The words quoted in the dedication to him still ring in my ears. At times of frustration I will lie in bed and think, "What would Dr. Ron say about this?"

Dr. Ron taught me two important lessons about medical science:

1. Doctors need to know what a child experiences in terms of symptoms—physically, behaviorally, and developmentally. He used to say, "I want to know what your whole day looks like. What patterns are there in how he reacts?" He taught me to glean information from Billy Ray's day-to-day functioning so he could track the patterns. He taught me what was important and what was not. This early training made possible the documentation system I have now developed and share in chapter 12.

2. You cannot always take every doctor's evaluation and treatment as appropriate. Dr. Ron helped me to see that no matter how superior a doctor's medical education may be, it is not feasible to cover every possibility for every patient. Some patients will respond differently to treatment or illnesses. When there are unusual combinations of diagnoses, treating an individual diagnosis becomes more cloudy and complicated.

Case in point: When Dr. Ron would be on vacation or on his day off, there was always a psychiatrist on call from the HMO, but it was rarely someone who knew Billy Ray or had access to his full chart. During one such time, Billy Ray's stimulant for ADHD had affected his appetite so much that his blood level of medication for bipolar disorder became toxic. The on-call doctor said to hold the medication for forty-eight hours and get another blood test. By the next day, Billy Ray had gone from being a sick little boy to totally out of control.

Dr. Ron told me that the on-call doctor was an excellent psychiatrist and in ninety-nine out of 100 patients, the advice would have been exactly right. But Billy Ray rapidly metabolized medication, so without repeated doses, the level of medication in his blood would drop too fast. Eventually Dr. Ron worked out a system where on his day off or when he was on vacation, I could call a specific doctor whom he had consulted with regarding Billy Ray's medication.

THERE'S NO "USUAL" WITH COMPLEX CHILDREN

I have come to hate the word *usual* when spoken by a professional of any kind. I have been told children *usually* do well on certain medications, *usually* develop at certain levels, *usually* show symptoms by a certain age, etc. Complex children are rarely usual.

Billy Ray's pediatrician, Dr. O'Brien, the most caring and sweetest lady you could ever hope to work with, told me several times during the first year following his seizures that most children who have a medication reaction such as this usually return to what was normal for them before the seizures. I clung to that hope for several years, while I watched him get worse instead of better. I truly believe the doctor held that same hope, because she cared so much for my son. When she retired five years later, we had to face together that we were never getting the old Billy Ray back. I think that realization was as painful for her as for me.

In sharing Billy Ray's medical history and experience with medications, you will notice that the specific drug is rarely named. The use of medications varies with the individual. For example, I recently read that a successful autistic person credits a certain medication with making a big difference in controlling nervous thinking. Interestingly enough, that same drug is the one believed to have caused the seizures that changed Billy Ray so completely, in fact bringing out his autistic symptoms. It is not my intention to steer you away from medications that might make a difference for your child.

As parents, we second-guess ourselves constantly. If the child had not been started on a certain medication, would things be different? We do what we think is best at the time. That is all that we can do. When Dr. Ron wanted to put Billy Ray on a medication that could cause serious side effects, Raymond and I were very concerned about doing that. Dr. Ron assured us that if we kept up the routine blood work, any problem could be caught early and reversed. In the end, we had to trust Dr. Ron and ourselves to evaluate the risks. Sometimes the risks do materialize. On the other hand, Billy Ray's behavior without the medication would probably have made him unmanageable at home. That was another risk, which we decided was more severe than the risk of him using the medication. Each new decision has to be evaluated.

Some parents swear by diet and natural remedies. It works very well for many children. We spent thousands of dollars that we could not afford to spend trying vitamins recommended by our pediatrician and a naturopathic physician. Billy Ray was unchanged by that attempt.

NEW MEDICATIONS: SPIN THE WHEEL

New medications and research are coming out constantly. Doctors have only the information provided to them. Sometimes new information on existing drugs is slow to get to practicing physicians. The medication believed to cause the seizures Billy Ray experienced is a case in point. Our urologist had been trying to get me to give Billy Ray that medication for an incontinence problem. He was on another medication, but the urologist felt that because he was on the top dosage, it would stop working as he grew and he would have a reoccurrence of the problem. For some reason, I was extremely reluctant to use that drug. Nothing in the literature substantiated my fears, but I resisted the change for two years.

Eventually school complaints caused us to look at changing Billy Ray's medication for ADHD. This same drug recommended for incontinence was suggested as an alternative to the drug he was using. I mentioned that the urologist had been suggesting it for a couple of years, but that for some reason I had been very reluctant. My present husband, Larry, is a whiz at finding information on the Internet. He found nothing that mentioned seizures as a risk. Neither the psychiatrist nor the pharmacist, both of whom I trusted completely, found any major risk. I decided I was being silly and acquiesced to trying it.

Probably six months to a year after Billy Ray's seizures, the psychiatrist told me that information about the drug's potential to lower the seizure threshold had been presented at a doctors' meeting. Our medical team—the psychiatrist, the pharmacist, my husband, and I—all did our homework. I also discussed it with the pediatrician even though she wasn't going to be prescribing it. Everyone felt it was safe. There was no way that any of us could have known the enormous damage to Billy Ray that would occur.

Over the years, many medications have been tried for Billy Ray. Some actually work for a honeymoon period and then appear to sort of turn on him. Others do not work at all. Others turn on him immediately.

CUTTING BACK ON SOME MEDICATIONS

Billy Ray seemed to be constantly physically ill when he was nineteen or twenty years old. He was on several psychiatric medications. Often by the time I could get enough medication in him to calm him down enough to take him to his doctors, he would literally sleep through the visits. Three of the medical doctors involved felt he was on too much psychiatric medication, but the psychiatrist was reluctant to discontinue the drugs.

I thought about the differing opinions among medical and psychiatric professionals. I watched him day after day while he was sick or sleeping all the time. He seemed to have no resistance to illness, suffering infections of multiple types at the same time. If he had enough medication to control his behavior completely, it generally kept him groggy or sleeping. I thought he was dying.

Removing him from the psychiatric medications involved risks. These were somewhat uncertain. However, I thought about his aggression. He is not self-abusive. The primary recipients of his aggression are his dog and me. If necessary, I was prepared to get rid of the dog and willing to put myself at risk to ascertain if discontinuing the medication would change his health. I bought him a funeral plan and fired the psychiatrist.

The mental-health coordinator threatened me with a child-abuse complaint. A rather nasty final summary was written that made me look like a terrible parent. He, in fact, did go to the county case manager. Fortunately, she was aware of the plan to stop using the psychiatrist and wean him off at least two of the drugs with the help of his pediatrician.

Our long-term pediatrician, Dr. O'Brien, was a specialist in developmental disabilities. Dr. Ruden, who inherited her practice, did not have that specialty. However, he has been there with me through the struggle to bring Billy Ray back to health. It has taken more than two years. Dr. Ruden listens to my concerns and we have worked together so well.

As we brought Billy Ray back to physical health, I continued to experiment in the way described in part two. Billy Ray is not medication-free by any means and probably never will be. He still gets an antiseizure medication that is used as a mood stabilizer (not for seizures), a mild ADHD medication, a sleep medication, and a medication for agitation that can be used on an as-needed basis. By creating his activities and environment in ways he best relates to, we are able to keep him on this reduced medication. Will it always be so? There is no way to be certain.

BECOMING AN EXPERT ON EXPERTS

I will always appreciate another psychiatrist (for reasons of his own he prefers to remain anonymous) who treated my son. I treasured his honesty in terms of admitting his own frustration at trying to figure out how to help Billy Ray. When I wrote him for permission to quote from some of his e-mail he responded:

> "Thanks so much for the update. Sounds like the Billy Ray saga goes on. I keep saying to people that I'd like to freeze myself for 100 years and come back when we know a lot more about brains and how they work—and what to do when they don't work right!
>
> "I like the book idea and have no problem at all with the quote. I would think the strength of your book would lie in its being honest in presenting how frustrating the struggle has been and how much experts often don't know. You could describe yourself as an expert on experts, I guess!"

Becoming "an expert on experts" is an undesirable title. The only way a parent becomes this is to have crisis after crisis taking the parent from one professional to another.

You learn a lot about the differences in style. Often it is more about style than skill. Sometimes the most caring doctors have a blunt or seemingly uncaring manner. Maybe they will stay with you through every struggle and be willing to look at every possibility, but they are not as friendly as others. You need to learn to relate to the expert just as much as you need to relate to your child. If you have faith in your doctor's skill, work to establish a relationship of mutual respect at a comfortable level for both of you.

MAKING SURE THE DOCTOR UNDERSTANDS YOUR CHILD

When Billy Ray is going to see a new doctor, I normally send past medical reports and an abbreviated history a week or so before the appointments. For the most part, doctors appreciate this preparation. However, occasionally they have not even glanced at the paperwork.

One specialist kept saying, "Just tell me." He was asking questions about medications tried when Billy Ray was five years old (he was by then eighteen years old). I finally asked this doctor to at least hand me the history that listed medications and results. I could not possibly remember all the history I had spent years preparing, which he had right in front of him but was refusing to look at. When I would try to answer him, he would cut me off almost immediately, so that I did not feel he was getting enough information to understand my son's condition. However, we left with a prescription for new medication. We saw this doctor three additional times. Each time he would ask questions, but not allow me time to answer adequately, and then he would do a quick check on my son. Each time he prescribed new medications; some caused frightening side effects that had not been explained to me. After the fourth visit, we did not take Billy Ray back to this doctor. We felt that without understanding my son's situation, his medication decisions were uninformed at best and maybe even dangerous given the side-effect potential.

Before choosing another doctor, it was clear we needed a system that could communicate the complex issues my son experienced in a compact format that a busy doctor could absorb clearly. If he or she was not willing to work with that, we could not rely on medical treatment recommended. (See chapter 12, "Document Everything," for the summary format I developed.)

The problems come in when a doctor cannot admit that he or she does not understand what is going on with your child. Your child may make that worse by acting differently in the doctor's office because of fear or stimulation. As in our case, the doctor may not have an accurate view of what goes on based on that difference in behavior. When you provide a brief summary that the professional can absorb quickly, he or she is able to see the problems better and have time left in the visit for examining the child and asking questions.

To get you started, I suggest that you begin honing your own instinct. Listen both with your ears and your gut to the doctor's opinion. If it does not sound accurate to you, don't hesitate to disagree, and explain why you feel the way you do. Never be afraid to say that you just do not feel right about the medication or the approach. If that does not work and you have tried to help the doctor to see things as they are, do not ever hesitate to take your child to another doctor. I do not mean to imply that you should argue with the doctor over every minor point. What I am referring to here are major issues, such as medication decisions, that strongly affect your child.

In most cases, you can work with a doctor. Try to build a relationship of mutual respect. The doctor must be someone whom you can communicate with and feel comfortable with. The doctor also must be someone who will listen to your instincts, which will become more reliable as time goes by. If that does not work, it may be time to find a new doctor.

HEALTH-CARE COVERAGE WOES

Insurance and health-care coverage through the government makes it difficult to even find an appropriate doctor or dentist. Billy Ray was covered under my insurance until he was out of my home and in a residential treatment center for restructuring his medications and evaluation. He became eligible for our state's health plan as a result. Once out of the treatment center and back in my home, he could get medical care through our HMO using the state's health plan, but he could no longer return to the psychiatrist he had before admission to the treatment center. Additionally, our HMO did not accept the state health plan for dental coverage. We loved the psychiatrist, and Billy Ray had the same pediatric dentist for sixteen years. Both were major losses.

The state health plan wanted us to choose an HMO dental plan. I started calling the plans they had given me to find dentists who had experience working with people with developmental disabilities. Of the three or four health-plan choices, none listed a dentist who had any experience with developmentally disabled patients. I got lists of dentists and spent three entire days calling dental offices. No dentists who would accept the coverage through the state health plan's HMO dental plans would agree to accept a child with autistic symptoms.

Finally, when I felt Billy Ray may have been experiencing a toothache, which was affecting his behavior, I decided to forget about whether a dentist would accept the state health plan coverage and just find a dentist that I would pay personally. I spent another day and a half on the telephone just trying to find a dentist who would see Billy Ray if we paid in cash. We did find a wonderful dentist near where we lived at that time, and she continued to take care of Billy Ray until we moved to another community.

After we moved, we considered whether we would stay with our wonderful pediatrician, which would mean driving three hours each way, or find a local doctor. I called every doctor the county developmental disabilities office recommended, plus some from the phone book and any recommendations I could get from anyone. Only one clinic would agree to accept the state health plan and Billy Ray's Medicare coverage.

SPECIAL PROBLEMS WITH DENTISTS

I understand that some dentists are afraid they will get punched or bitten by complex children. Sometimes they will perform the work only if the patient is sedated. Certainly, dentists have a right to refuse to work on patients they feel uncomfortable with. By their not accepting that type of patient before the patient comes in, the child is not embarrassed. In terms of sedation, I ask that a dentist give Billy Ray a chance to show that he will cooperate before we discuss sedation. If the dentist is not willing to try, I choose another dentist.

Because of the move, we had to search for a new dentist. I saw the dentist first for my own teeth and spoke to him about Billy Ray. In fact, I saw him two days before Billy Ray's appointment. I brought his x-rays and explained that the pediatrician had ordered an extra amount of his as-needed medication for agitation if we needed it for dental appointments, but we rarely did. I explained that Billy Ray had a wonderful pediatric dentist as a child, so he felt safe in a dental chair. I said occasionally a bite block is needed to help him remember to keep his mouth open but overall he is very cooperative.

The day of Billy Ray's dental appointment, the assistant seated him without problem. The dentist came in, didn't say hello or introduce himself, and just said, "I am going to put the chair down." He lowered the back of the chair and immediately told me he was referring Billy Ray to a specialist because he would never be able to get him to keep his mouth open. That appeared to be total bias not based on fact, because he did not even ask Billy Ray to open his mouth and made no attempt to even look in his mouth. It felt like he had made up his mind before he walked into the room. Billy Ray was quite confused. He kept saying, "Dentist no open mouth. We go back."

CHAPTER 6

ENCOUNTERING THE
"DUMB-PARENT TREATMENT"

SERVICES TO A DISABLED CHILD are generally handled by a
team. This usually includes educational professionals, such as the director
of special education for the local school district, the speech therapist,
vision specialist, recreation/vocational therapist, autism or behavior therapist, teacher(s), and parents or guardians. Depending on where you live
and what other services your child receives, the team might also include
a county case manager and other providers of service to your child.

The team creates an Individual Education Plan (IEP) or Individual
Service Plan (ISP). These plans contain goals and the services needed to
reach those goals. Many goals are based on testing done by the various
professionals. For example, the speech therapist may give a report about
her work with the child and recommend speech goals. If the team agrees

with these recommendations, they become a goal. Parents make requests for certain skills to be taught. If the team agrees that those skills are appropriate, they become a goal as well.

Because parents are with their children much more than anyone, you would think that they would be the most respected members of the team. Professionals will often pay lip service to this concept, saying, "Parents know their children best," or that parents are "the leaders of the team." When I hear these words, I think of something Billy Ray often says: "Yeah right." Parents are not always treated with the respect they deserve. I have seen firsthand the difference in the way parents are treated and the way professionals are treated.

Lack of respect for parents as the leaders of the team appears to be an international problem. My e-mail program has a file of correspondence from parents in many countries, who shared similar experiences of disrespect by professionals, especially in the education system.

The "dumb-parent treatment" is an unspoken attitude that seems to imply parents do not understand their children or that parents' opinions are unimportant. If the parent sees the child as functioning at a higher level than the school or the physician does, then the parent is not viewing the child objectively. It can be conveyed subtly or not so subtly, but the attitude says you are only a dumb parent who does not know anything. How dare you question the opinions of professionals? It is something most parents will deal with at some point in their children's lives. It is not necessarily about the parent's intelligence or sophistication. I have spoken with professionals in various fields who were treated similarly when they attended meetings regarding their own children.

OUR FIRST "DUMB-PARENT" EXPERIENCE

Within the first two weeks following my son's adoptive placement, we had our first experience with the "dumb-parent treatment."

Billy Ray was not yet walking when he came to us at fifteen months old. My parents had purchased a walker to be passed down among the grandchildren. My brother's three children had already used it. Almost immediately, after my Dad put Billy Ray in the walker and worked with him in it, he was literally running in it. We were all delighted.

The early intervention specialist came to our home the second week Billy Ray was with us. The first words out of her mouth were, "You shouldn't have him in that walker." According to her, it would negatively affect his balance in the future and it might affect his gait as an adult. Emotions of shame immediately welled up. I thought I should pull him out of the walker immediately but did not. Fortunately, the walker issue became a moot point. Having run in it for a week, it motivated him to walk. Maybe we weren't such dumb parents after all.

A DRAWN-OUT BATTLE OVER TESTING

Our school district eventually got Billy Ray into a combination program of Head Start and specialized preschool. He was tested upon entering the program. Our HMO specialists evaluated him as well. His performance on intelligence and other tests was not nearly equal to his performance at home.

When I would hear the results of testing done with him that showed he couldn't recognize numbers or words or even animals and could only count to two, I would describe how he functioned at home. The reaction was usually that I was helping him too much or that I was not able to be objective. The message seemed to be, "You are only the parent, what do you know?"

I started refusing consent for any testing except that done by his own classroom teacher, with whom he was very familiar. His teacher shared with me that she knew he could do many of the things he did not do while being tested. At IEP meetings, many of the goals were created based on Billy Ray's performance in tests. I argued that this was unfair. He was able to do substantially better absent the stress of testing. I felt he needed to be allowed to reach for goals based on performance not connected with testing.

Requests for consent to do testing continued to come and I continued to refuse, stating that it gave an unrealistic view of his functioning. Although they needed parental consents to do the testing, they did not accept my refusal to consent to the testing. It seemed like a violation of my rights as a parent.

Threatening letters came with copies of the journal pages that I sent back and forth to the classroom teacher. I felt totally betrayed because I believed that the teacher understood and agreed with my position.

Conflict with program administrators continued through Billy Ray's three-year placement in the multihandicapped preschool and Head Start because I resisted testing. In my opinion, Billy Ray did not accomplish as much as he could have because we never got past this conflict and into developing a program that worked for him.

RESPECT AS A PROFESSIONAL, NOT AS A PARENT

I started a small fiduciary business while Billy Ray was in elementary school. I had guardianship clients with different diagnoses and situations. Whether clients were in nursing homes, vocational programs, foster homes, etc., there were generally planning meetings comparable to the IEP meetings for my son.

It did not take long to notice the difference in the respect I received as a professional guardian as opposed to how I was treated in meetings as Billy Ray's mother. I struggled with trying to figure out what I might be doing differently regarding clients. It seemed that as parent I should have more influence than as a professional guardian who saw her clients less than the child living in my own home.

Initially I questioned my own objectivity regarding Billy Ray. Were my expectations higher for him than for my clients? Did I refuse to accept his limitations? With a great deal of soul-searching, it became apparent that I did become defensive and angry in meetings regarding Billy Ray. To increase confidence, I began being more prepared with documentation and notes to keep my focus in meetings.

During the time I was examining my own advocacy skills, I was appointed guardian for a client with autism. That diagnosis was unfamiliar to me at that time. To ensure that the client had appropriate services, I hired an independent case manager to assist in planning for him. After reviewing her report and my own involvement, I decided I was going to get him out of the large state institution where he resided. I set about creating a plan and asked for a meeting.

The case manager and I walked into a large room with maybe twenty professionals; Our job that day was to demonstrate why my client should be placed on the community transition list. I was a bit intimidated, because I was inexperienced at that time. About ninety minutes later, we walked out of the room with an agreement to move my client to a community setting near my home office. The case manager looked at me and said, "If I ever need an advocate, I hope you are available."

Driving back to the office, I thought about that meeting. I had expected it to be an uphill battle. I had strongly prepared and was assertive, not aggressive. I felt respected and listened to. I compared that to the IEP meeting for my own son the prior week, where I had felt so belittled and lost my cool. I was the same person. My knowledge of my son was greater than that of a client I had known only a few months and never seen outside of the institution.

It finally became apparent that in terms of clients, I could review notes from my visits with the clients and those involved in whatever program and make a list of important issues. After listening to the report given, I could disagree and my position was considered. Others might add more information that resolved the disagreement. If we still did not agree, generally my position as guardian was respected. For the most part, my goals for clients became a part of the plan, and those I disagreed with did not.

I could leave one of those meetings where I had been listened to wearing the same outfit and the same perfume and carrying the same briefcase to an IEP meeting for my son. I would start out listening to the reports. The first time questions were asked, the sense of "How dare you question professional educators, you're only the dumb parent!" was communicated by attitude and/or body language. Comments about my lack of objectivity were common. My own requests and suggestions were rarely incorporated into the goals. I left most meetings feeling defeated and embarrassed at how defensive I had become.

TIME FOR A CHANGE

Once I became angry or defensive, the process of trying to come to some agreement regarding appropriate planning for Billy Ray really stopped. The victim of this process was my son. Nothing was being accomplished to help him as long as we were stuck in the power struggle that occurred every time we had planning meetings. It seemed imperative that the problem be addressed so that Billy Ray was able to have a realistic plan.

I recently watched a video prepared by well-known consultant Dan Hobbs. Describing the parent in his case, he said that she was quite knowledgeable about her child. He said she was made to look like a bad person when the professionals failed with her child. This made so much sense in the context of my own experience. If the professionals do not know how to help a client, it is so much easier to blame the parents than to admit their own failure. If the parent gets angry and defensive, it provides an explanation they can use to explain why the child is not succeeding—the parent is difficult or uncooperative.

I have read several books that attribute this tension among professionals, team members, and parents to the parents' denial, grief, or disappointment in accepting the limitations of their children. That may be true in certain cases. The frustration a parent feels at not being respected as a parent and the leader on the child's team is also a factor. This frustration creates a sense of powerlessness and anger. You will need to look at your reactions and try to ascertain what is applicable to you.

However, there are some cases where the "dumb-parent treatment" is taken to an entirely different level—beyond an attitude of disrespect to the threat of reprisal if you don't back off.

A HORROR STORY

Following Billy Ray's medication reaction that brought out autistic-like symptoms, I met with a new teacher for my son. I explained that he was showing the "rub-off touch": if you would bump him or touch his arm, he would touch his arm then pretend to rub the touch back on you. He would even do that with the dog if she brushed against him or the car door if he bumped into it. Most of the time his personality was more outgoing and he was fine with being touched, but he was inconsistent. I also explained that he had been scratching himself a lot, and that we were looking into potential allergies with the pediatrician. So far, she had been unable to find a reason. We had changed soaps and other products to no avail. The teacher understood those issues and said they were common.

Very early in the school year, I received a telephone call from one of the professionals who would regularly go into my son's classroom. The call caused me to have concerns about Billy Ray's classroom environment. I made some unexpected visits to the room and spent time listening out of sight in the hall. I heard some things I wasn't comfortable with and referred my concerns to the director of special education.

Approximately two weeks after my conversation with the director, my doorbell rang just before it was time for Billy Ray to come home from school. There stood a uniformed deputy and a protective-services caseworker. I did not say hello before I asked if Billy Ray was okay. I imagined a bus wreck or something equally terrible had happened. They said that he was fine, but they had received a child-abuse complaint from the school. The report alleged that he had numerous scratches on his body and that he was reluctant to be touched.

Having been a transcriber in the same state agency years before, I knew that uniformed officers do not generally accompany caseworkers unless they plan to remove a child from the home. I was so frightened by the idea of losing Billy Ray, I could barely speak. Somehow, I managed to explain the autistic symptoms about touch that he occasionally showed and how we had battled with self-scratching for years.

When Billy Ray came home from school, he was mortified. He and his deceased dad had watched the television show *COPS* for many years. The theme song "Bad Boys" meant to Billy Ray that cops only come after bad boys. I was horrified that he would be taken from me, but he was afraid he was going to jail. I told him that the men were worried about scratches on his chest and back. I pulled his shirt off so that they could see. There were three or four old-looking, very light marks on his chest. The protective-services worker asked him how he got those marks on his chest. Billy Ray held up his hands and said, "Nails."

The caseworker handed me his card and said he would be investigating the matter further. I gave him the pediatrician's name and telephone number to verify what I told him. I kept checking with the pediatrician, who said the caseworker had not even called her. She assured me that the matter would be fine once she talked to the caseworker, but I still worried day and night. A week later, I telephoned the caseworker only to find out that he was on vacation for three weeks. Almost a month after their profoundly disturbing visit, I finally reached the caseworker by telephone. He said that he had listed it as "unfounded" the same day he saw my son. He further said that he could not tell me whether the teacher had been warned in this case, but in some cases when there is a malicious complaint, the complainant is warned that it is a criminal offense.

Since that time, I have heard of other families who have experienced the terror of unfounded child-abuse complaints. Some have felt, as I did, that the complaints were communicating that we should back off from power struggles regarding our children.

DOCTORS DO IT TOO

The "dumb-parent treatment" is probably more frequent within school systems dealing with IEPs, but I have personally experienced it with medical and psychiatric personnel as well.

A few years ago, my son had to have some minor surgery to lance a cyst on his leg. I sent the caregiving assistant to a nearby store to pick up loose-fitting sweatpants for him to wear home, because we were not prepared for the surgery and it would have taken too long to go home for them. In the meantime, Billy Ray and I were called into the room. The young surgery resident introduced himself and asked if I was Mom. I asked him several questions about what he was going to do and what he was finding once he started the procedure. He either did not respond at all or was abrupt in his response. In the middle of the surgery, the caregiving assistant was shown into the room. I introduced her to the surgeon as someone who assisted me with Billy Ray's care. He immediately stopped the process and explained to her what he had found and what was involved in the procedure. Here was my employee (whom I had trained) being treated as the person to be dealt with, and I, the parent, was unimportant.

After Billy Ray's seizures, the psychiatrist tried many different medication combinations to try to stabilize him. Finally, he insisted that Billy Ray be put in a residential treatment center where he could be constantly monitored while having his medication restructured.

During my conversations with the director of the treatment center, he told me that parents often disappear once they put their children in the center. The facility has a gigantic waiting list that can be rearranged by severity of the child's needs. I thought it was a real possibility that the parents had simply burned out by the time they got their children into the center. However, once I had my son in placement there, I saw that it might not be as much about parent burnout as about the "dumb-parent treatment" they received.

One day I walked into the office for a meeting about my son. Another meeting was going on, so I waited in the entry area. Posted over the photocopier was a flyer for mandatory staff training on "dealing with difficult case managers, parents, and guardians." That gave me some insight into the attitude toward parents getting involved.

The psychiatrist for the center was very difficult to work with. I had been a bit hesitant to work with this doctor before admission because of stories I had heard. However, he was someone our psychiatrist was familiar with and our doctor assured me he would be fine. I felt like I was an experienced advocate and, as such, I could deal with whatever came. I was wrong. Everything I said was discounted. Reports made me look neurotic.

While on a weekend pass, Billy Ray made allegations of abuse at the center. I will not elaborate, because we were never able to prove them. I had contact with the center director by e-mail immediately. The psychiatrist was apparently there when I returned my son, and he wrote a report insinuating that the alleged abuse had happened at home. As with the teacher's unfounded allegation of child abuse, I felt the report communicated to me that I should back off.

TAKING CONTROL

I thought about the difference in respect I received as a professional guardian and as a parent. I made a list of the kinds of steps I might take when planning for the care of a new client. One of the first things I might do for a client would be to get an evaluation by a professional pertinent to the particular client's needs. Armed with this report, I would attend relevant meetings and advocate my client's needs, helping arrange a plan that best suited my client.

I considered getting an independent evaluation for Billy Ray. The cost would have been thousands of dollars. Many evaluations had been done through the school district and our HMO, as well as substantial medical tests. We knew a lot about what was not creating his problems in school and behavior issues at home. I decided that because he historically performed at a higher level at home than at school or during testing, I would start by doing some experimentation at home.

Before I started experimenting, I tried hard to look at his best years and worst years in terms of happiness and learning. Billy Ray has experienced four exceptionally good years and two very difficult years that really stood out in my mind. Looking back on those years, I found significant patterns.

A VERY GOOD YEAR

During seventh grade, Billy Ray and I moved to a small community with Larry. I did not like moving him in the middle of a year, but a gang was threatening us in our neighborhood in the city. We had a meeting with the new school staff that would be working with Billy Ray.

Following the meeting, the special-education teacher visited Billy Ray in his existing classroom. Our existing school district had three-year "learning centers," and Billy Ray was in his second year there. The district had decided to make the classroom for children with severe behavior problems. Billy Ray was stable enough on medications that he did not need to be in that type of classroom, but the district did not remove the existing students. Like many kids, Billy Ray tended to copy the behavior of those around him. So when the new teacher visited his prior classroom, she saw him engaging in bad behavior.

I received a call from the director of special education in the new district during Christmas break. He said that the new teacher did not feel Billy Ray would fit into her classroom. He requested an extra week following Christmas break to get a specialized program worked out for Billy Ray. Billy Ray was to be in the resource room and have a one-to-one assistant.

I went for a meeting with the teacher in that arrangement, Connie. We talked at length about what Billy Ray did at home and what he was capable of doing. Connie created a wonderful program for him. He was included in three regular classrooms with adaptive assignments. She even had him play a practice drum with the band. Besides academics, he enjoyed working in the cafeteria and pulling weeds with the janitor. He had his own locker and felt like a real part of the school. Every day he went to the school office to greet either the principal or vice principal, as well as the secretaries. He had never been happier or able to do more than during the rest of that year, and it continued in the summer. His self-confidence bloomed.

A VERY BAD YEAR

The next year the school district made a budget mistake, so they pulled the one-to-one aide. Billy Ray would not have been able to function in the resource-room placement and three regular classrooms without his aide. Connie and I both advocated to the school superintendent to restore the aide. I was told he would be given an aide for at least the first few months.

Without consulting me first, Billy Ray was placed in the classroom of the teacher who had refused to have him the prior year. I spoke with the teacher (we will call her Wanda), who was quite open about the fact that because she would have lost one of her aides, she decided to incorporate Billy Ray into her class. She was surprised that I would object to his placement in her room. I made it quite clear that the superintendent had promised an aide for a few months until Billy Ray could be taught his new schedule. I would agree to place him in her room only if he would be allowed to go to the three regular classes he was included in and if he could continue to eat in the cafeteria with friends he had established. Wanda agreed; however, she told me most of her parents begged her to keep her students out of the regular student population because of bad language and other habits they picked up.

Billy Ray showed signs of reduced self-esteem almost immediately. We were not having behavioral issues at home, but his joy was gone. I called Wanda to check in. I learned that he was not going to the three regular classes because "He didn't get enough out of it to make it worth taking one of my aides out of the class for a whole period." In addition, he was not eating in the cafeteria. If he did that, one of her aides would have to lose his or her lunchtime, according to Wanda. None of the other parents wanted their children to eat in the cafeteria.

Soon I started getting calls from the speech therapist and other parents praising Wanda's work with my son and other children, urging me not to go forward with an attempt to have him removed from Wanda's classroom. If I did that, they told me, Wanda would lose the aide the superintendent had agreed to pull from her room to work with Billy Ray in the resource room. I spoke to Connie about it. She encouraged me to let it slide because I probably couldn't win. If I got Billy Ray out of the class with one of Wanda's aides, it would be a constant struggle with Wanda trying to get the aide back, and Billy Ray and the aide probably would end up back there. Billy Ray would be going to high school the next year, so we should just try to get through.

I started getting wonderful notes about how well Billy Ray was doing, and he was bringing home very well-done craft projects. Within a week of the "good notes," Wanda called me at dinnertime just before the first school board meeting of the year. Apparently, her program was being threatened. She was concerned it would be shut down and all the kids would be placed in an inclusion program. She wanted me to go to the board meeting and speak up for her program. I told her the best thing I could do is stay away from the board meeting. If I went, I would testify in favor of closing the self-contained classroom. I had seen the way my son, the child she felt was too low functioning to be in her classroom the prior year, had bloomed with more inclusion. Almost immediately after that board meeting, I started getting "bad notes" about Billy Ray's hyperactivity every day.

The bad notes would continue until shortly before the next school board meeting, then good notes would reappear, and she would start calling at dinnertime again. Parents were calling too. I asked them where they got the telephone number and one said from the teacher. I confronted Wanda about giving out my number and she denied giving it to anyone. However, one day I picked Billy Ray up early and found she had my home and business telephone numbers taped to her desk where anyone could see it. No other parents' numbers were there—just ours.

Wanda's complaints about hyperactivity continued. Larry and I discussed her complaints and the fact that we were not experiencing behavior other than a normal kid in adolescence might experience. Larry made a list of behaviors and we went in to discuss it with the psychiatrist. I did not have experience to know as much as the men, both fathers who had

had teenage boys. Larry compared Billy Ray to his sons at the same age and found similarity. The psychiatrist did say that Billy Ray had been on the same stimulant for much longer than is recommended. He also noted that ADHD could be present at school but not at home. His recommendation was to change medications. As described earlier, we eventually changed to the medication that is felt to have caused the seizures that changed Billy Ray into a complex child.

I could go on and on about this teacher's agenda. The truth is that the child who was too low functioning for her classroom the year before had bloomed with inclusion. He failed miserably in her classroom even before the seizures in February of that school year. The following year, Billy Ray went on to high school. Wanda's totally isolated classroom was closed, and her students were put in a program with more inclusion. I don't know what happened to Wanda.

THE OVERALL PATTERNS

Billy Ray's freshman year was better for him than the prior year, but the "dumb-parent treatment" got in the way of much success. His sophomore year was spent in the classroom of the teacher who made the child-abuse complaint. That was a horrible year as well.

There is a definite pattern to his successful years. They were with teachers willing to adapt to his needs, who created in Billy Ray a sense of belonging to his class and to the school in general. Both teachers were eager to work with parents to give their students the highest degree of success.

I already told you how Billy Ray thrived in seventh grade working with Connie. For kindergarten through second grade, Billy Ray had a teacher, Mary, who recognized the value of parental input. We worked well as a team. She told me the first time we met that these kids were not just a job to her, they were her life. She taught Billy Ray so much. He learned to recognize his name and other words partly because every day Mary had each student come to the head of the room, find his or her own name, and say his or her address. When I told her that I believed he was sight reading from all the reading we had done at home and that he was recognizing signs or advertising on trucks from television commercials, she believed me.

In the two worst years, both teachers had their own agendas and were vindictive. Billy Ray's self-esteem was damaged as a result. I am not certain how much advocating on my part could have changed either teacher's attitude. However, when your child is having his self-esteem improved by successful activities at home and you are able to demonstrate his capabilities to the team in general, it at least can give you some evidence to help you overcome the "dumb-parent treatment."

ADVOCACY IS NOT WAGING WAR

The program manager in one school district told me the district's relationship with parents is hampered by the risk of lawsuits. Educational professionals are on edge fearing lawsuits. Some parents are so frustrated when services are inappropriate that they threaten to sue, which puts more stress on the relationship.

The "dumb-parent treatment" is demeaning and makes us angry. We have reason to be fighting mad. When we go with that, however, the real victims are our children. The war really becomes more about defending yourself, and your child is left out of it. All this fighting takes valuable time that could be spent making things better for your child. True advocacy is team building and working together for the benefit of the child. Fighting might win the battle, but lose the war.

I determined that if I got stuck in another "dumb-parent-treatment" situation, I would not hesitate to work with the director of special education to resolve it. I created the following goals to turn things around for Billy Ray:

- In order to advocate for him, I would step back and take a closer look at my son. I would have to be sure of his strengths and weaknesses. I needed to really get to know my child again and really try to bring to the surface what was so familiar to me that I did not think about anymore.

- I would try to bring past successes into the present and avoid these problems in the future.

- I would deal with personal issues that caused me to get defensive. As a professional, I realized that I was able to handle hostile situations without becoming nearly as reactive as I was to Billy Ray's situation.

Parents should not have to prove their expertise relative to their own children or earn the respect, but I was determined to do that if that is what was necessary. The process of demonstrating your expertise has the side benefit of making you feel more confident too. We will talk more about this in chapter 13, "Getting the Professionals to Listen."

CHANGING COURSE
Solutions and Suggestions

ALL PARENTS HAVE REGRETS. If only I had done this or not done that. If only I had known. Whether your child is two months or twenty-three years old, it is not too late to help him have the best life possible. Start where you are. Don't make unattainable goals for either your child or yourself. Do the best that you can for your child and be content with that.

7

TURNING POINT

TURNING POINTS COME for all of us in our own ways. We respond in our unique ways just as our children respond in their own ways to stimulation. Something inside pulls us into a deeper reality of where we are and what we need to go on. In our lives, there was increasing hopelessness about Billy Ray's future. I had put all I could give into my son, and it was not working.

Turning points come at different points in our lives. I wish so many times that ours had come much sooner. The things we learned would have made a difference in Billy Ray's early years, though he was less complex then. The reason the turning point came so late for us was that Billy Ray's crisis occurred at fourteen years old. Facing the permanence of his situation was delayed because the pediatrician and I hoped that he eventually would return to what was normal for him, as most children in such cases do. Six months after the medication reaction, she said that sometimes it takes longer. We clung to that hope for three years.

Little time had been devoted to anything but Billy Ray since his health crisis. I had totally lost touch with my faith, my business had failed, and I was in a somewhat desperate situation apart from Billy Ray's problems. And Billy Ray was still not doing well.

I was tired of hearing what a great parent I was to stay with my son. Our pediatrician once stated that many adoptive parents would have given up in the early years. That was not something I ever seriously considered, but I found it unacceptable that we could not do more for him despite his dubious title as "one of the most complicated cases." The regular reminder of "doing the best you can under the circumstances" was not comforting. I longed for some sort of peace in our lives instead of the constant struggle to survive day to day.

I had taken Billy Ray to every specialist I could, tried all recommendations—including ones I had doubts about or had tried before—and done everything I could think of myself. He was still yelling, bouncing up and down, punching me, refusing to go to school much of the time, and having major sleep problems.

His symptoms of autism, which I recognized from my autistic clients, were increasing. Both his pediatrician and his psychiatrist said he was probably not autistic, because he did not develop symptoms until puberty, following the seizures. In the autism evaluation report, the autism specialist said Billy Ray had symptoms comparable to those of autism spectrum disorder (ASD) in the severe range. The neurologist was saying he disagreed with a diagnosis of autism and that it could be the dementia that sometimes afflicts folks who experience Down syndrome.

The worst part was blaming myself for giving him the medication that caused the seizures that changed Billy Ray so dramatically. My instinct had made me hesitant to use that medication, and I had resisted it for two years. I finally agreed because nothing in the research or professional opinions gave any indication of this severe reaction as a risk. I felt I had ruined my son's life and could never make it right.

Professionals whom I trusted were repeatedly suggesting out-of-home placement. Instead of saying it would be best for Billy Ray, the reason given most of the time was that it would be better for me or that I would have to place him eventually, so why not save some life for myself. I knew what it would mean in Billy Ray's life, because he had been in placement for nine months. Additionally, because of my work, I had experience with many types of facilities. Billy Ray's uniqueness would make it difficult for him to fit in at most facilities.

The final straw came when one of the doctors mentioned that shock therapy was again being used for complicated cases where medications failed to adequately control behavior. I bristled and responded, "Not in my lifetime." Driving home from that doctor's office, I realized that my lifetime was not going to be enough if we did not turn things around for Billy Ray now.

SEEKING PEACE

Crisis has a way of turning us toward our personal faith. In time of national tragedy or crisis, politicians routinely encourage prayer, even if that is not something they would normally do. I had been so busy trying to fix my son and juggle other demands, I had lost focus with my personal beliefs. When I realized this, I returned to my faith. (A more detailed description of my spiritual journey as it relates to parenting my son is being written in a separate book. If you want to read more about my personal spiritual approach to parenting, you may also go to my other website: www.lighthouseparents.com.)

The Serenity Prayer kept ringing in my ears:

God grant me the serenity to accept the things I cannot change,
Courage to change the things I can,
And wisdom to know the difference.

That little prayer really is profound. We can change many things for the good of our children. We can't change some things. Knowing the difference is a difficult balance to find. We do need wisdom to understand the difference.

We needed peace on all battlefields not just for Billy Ray, but for us, his parents, as well. We realized:

- There would be no peace for Billy Ray until we could find a better way of communicating with him. His frustration would decrease if his needs were understood.

- That communication had to be used to adapt his life to a more comfortable routine.

- The "dumb-parent treatment" had to stop. The goals for Billy Ray could be accomplished only through becoming part of a true team. Anger, no matter how justified, must be avoided, and a determined attempt must be made to work within the system.

- We needed community leisure and lifestyle activities to be peaceful and pleasant.

- A plan for Billy Ray's future, even if I was no longer able to take care of him, had to be formulated.

That was a lot to be accomplished—how could it be done? I sought wisdom from God and others.

ADOPTING A PRACTICAL APPROACH

If you were the CEO of a big company, you would periodically look at how the company was doing. You would look at the policies and procedures that make your staff happy and productive. If certain procedures are followed, the staff will be happier and will produce more profit. You also have to look at what would make you, the boss, happy enough to want to stay in that position.

If the company were a manufacturing plant and production was not where you wanted it, you might hire an efficiency expert to look closely at how the production is done and determine if there is a better way to do the same tasks with greater productivity.

Part two asks you to step back and look at things like a CEO might. You need to look at things as objectively and realistically as possible. The observing and experimenting will help you to do that.

This requires some work on your part. To motivate yourself to spend your limited energy on the suggested tasks, think about how you would like things to be for your child. Do not forget to think about what would make you and the rest of the family happier too. This will help you to stay with it when you are tempted to give up and either isolate your child and the family in survival mode or place your child out of the home before you are ready to do that. Set some attainable goals, such as:

- I will walk out of an IEP meeting feeling that something has been accomplished for my child's benefit.
- He will achieve educational goals that are reasonable for his abilities.
- He will be less agitated.
- His general well-being will be the best it can be.
- I will make some time to address the needs of my other children and my spouse.

Allow yourself some goals that may seem silly to others who take certain pleasures for granted in their daily lives, such as:

- I will make some time for myself.
- I will make time for a peaceful cup of coffee every morning.
- I will make time for my own medical and dental care.

This process with Billy Ray was definitely bootstrap learning. We started backward, but it worked for us. It gave me hope that we really could turn things in a better direction.

BOOTSTRAP LEARNING

The case manager for the state program that helped us with in-home staff made various programs used for treating autism available to me and provided an in-home consultant. Both the case manager and the consultant saw autism tendencies in Billy Ray. The consultant was the same person I had hired for my two autistic clients, which helped tremendously because I was already comfortable with her. I certainly saw some similarity to my clients, but Billy Ray seemed more complicated than they did.

We tried various approaches suggested in the materials provided by the case manager, together with volumes of Internet research my husband printed out and every book I could find on autism, especially Temple Grandin's work. We also researched other disabilities and looked at approaches for those. Billy Ray lived through much frustration as we tried various approaches that didn't work for him.

Because none of the approaches, even when done exactly as recommended, were working, I started looking at what had worked before and after Billy Ray's crisis. Then I combined many of those things with parts of the approaches that weren't working and started again.

I wanted to discover why he could maintain attention and control his behavior (making noise, bouncing up and down, throwing things, destroying property, and occasional aggression) long enough to feed the horses or do certain other activities. I kept saying to the pediatrician, the psychiatrist, and the educational professionals, "If only we could figure out how to bring this motivation to control his behavior into the rest of his life, he'd be happier and need less medication." I was told it was a fluke or that he could control himself for the five-minute task of feeding the horses but not for the rest of his day.

In addition to feeding the horses well at home, he had experienced his best year in school just before he had the medication reaction. I thought about the kinds of things that his teacher had created for him that year. At the beginning of the next year, he had some of the same activities but had behavior issues at school. I wrote down everything that was involved in his most successful year and the changes the next year, before the medication reaction in February.

It was easy to see that although both teachers gave him academic and hands-on instruction in various life skills, including social skills, the first teacher involved peer tutors and brought him out into the general school population. She had projects he could do with the janitor, for example, as opposed to doing everything in the self-contained classroom the other teacher maintained. He loved to wash tables in the cafeteria, but he was not cooperative with the same task in the self-contained classroom. The first teacher made him feel like he was a part of the school, while the other teacher had a strong aversion to inclusion or mainstreaming. Billy Ray thrived on the inclusion and regressed in the isolation of a self-contained classroom.

One thing he had enjoyed was having his own briefcase to carry around when he accompanied me to visit clients. In Billy Ray's most successful year, his teacher had used the briefcase more as a planner. I took the software we used for making symbols and started making schedules, which were inserted into the planner. Billy Ray was somewhat responsive to those but was not particularly excited about them.

To my amazement, the software had symbols for profanity and sex but none for caregivers or routine activities that I wanted to use for his schedules. So I took pictures with my 35 mm camera and had them developed and put on CD to make symbols for Billy Ray. Eventually a friend offered a digital camera she seldom used. Including these pictures made all the difference in our ability to make Billy Ray's schedules. His response to the schedules that had actual pictures of him doing an activity or of specific people was much better than it had been to the symbols. After noticing this, I took pictures of every activity he did and created all his schedules with digital pictures. We were on our way. It was the jump start we needed.

I knew that he might never function as well as he had functioned both at home and at school during that year with the teacher who believed in inclusion so strongly. However, because I had seen the difference in his behavior in the second classroom, even before his medical situation, I thought there was a chance we could get back some of the happy, high-functioning Billy Ray. I was determined to try.

The most important themes of this book are adapting and communicating. In order to adapt your child's life to his abilities and comfort level, you need to first learn from him as much as you can. Thus, chapter 8 is titled "The Best Teacher—Your Child." As you read and try the suggestions, keep in mind anything you notice that might be adapted to work better for you and your child. Note it in your journal.

THE BEST TEACHER— YOUR CHILD

THE RELATIONSHIP BETWEEN parent(s) and children is like no other. You know your child better than anyone does. There are things you know about her that are so familiar you may not even think about them. Some of the very answers you seek are right there in your memory. For purposes of this chapter, we will try to tap into that memory and your power of observation.

No one has a better opportunity to know a child than the parents she lives with. She will perform better for you because she feels comfortable. Unfortunately, she will also show you negative behaviors that she would never feel safe acting out in public. Much of getting to know her happens just by being with her day in and day out.

Discovering simple changes in your approach can make a big difference for your child. You will wonder how you never noticed these things before. Operating in survival mode, trying to take care of your child, and fighting the system to get her needs met is exhausting. When trying to get through the day-to-day survival, it is easy to miss things. Try not to get stuck on what you should have known. Just start where you and your child are today.

CHARTING A TYPICAL DAY

It will help to have an overview of your child's typical day from your viewpoint—before you start keeping a detailed journal of the events of each day. Once you get into keeping a daily journal, you may be surprised by some of the things you discover.

Get some paper or start a computer document to make notes and answer the following questions about what a normal day for your child is now:

- What time does he wake up? How many hours sleep does that generally mean?

- Is it interrupted sleep or straight through the night?

- List any comments about sleep that you want to remember for later:

  - What kind of mood does your child wake in? Does he seem oriented or disoriented?

  - What is the first question or communication by behavior your child makes in the morning? For example, Billy Ray always asks, "Where are we going?" immediately before going to sleep and the minute he wakes up. This observation will help you to determine what is important to your child about his day.

- List the events of a normal day for your child in the order they occur. If he goes to school or another day program, list from waking up to going to school and from arriving home to going back to sleep.

- List stressful times that appear consistently in his day. For example, note if he consistently has trouble transitioning to and from the school bus, bath time, or other specific activities.

- Write down any areas about your child's schedule or problem areas that you want to observe extra closely for possible modification later. Keep this list handy in your notebook so that you can make notes as you go along.

KEEPING A DAILY JOURNAL

This is not a scientific evaluation. By taking a closer look at day-to-day things, you are more likely to be able to adapt schedules, approaches, and environments to your child's needs. You will learn much by spending the time you already spend with your child. Watch a little closer than normal how he reacts to activities, tasks, or stimulation. There may be ways to interact with him or structure approaches that come to you while observing. At this point just make note of those rather than try to change anything.

Figure 8.1 is an example of what entries in a basic journal might look like.

Start your own journal in some format comfortable for you, such as on your computer or in a notebook. If you choose a notebook, I would recommend a three-ring binder rather than a bound journal or spiral notebook, so you can put the forms and checklists in as you go along.

Do not try to rely on your memory. If you keep notes, you are more likely to catch patterns of responses and behaviors that you might miss by depending on your memory. When you look at your notes later, sometimes it is like a light dawning in your head when you see something that didn't occur to you at the time you were going through the event with your child.

For a couple of weeks or even a month, just be a little extra observant and write down exactly what you see. In your journal, note things such as:

- Behavior that is bothersome. Note what your child was doing just before the behavior occurred or if he appeared upset over anything. Include reports from the school unless you have a carry-

FIGURE 8.1   Sample daily journal entry.

JOURNAL FOR 2/10/05 through _____	
DATE	**COMMENTS**
2/10/05	Woke up 12 p.m., back to sleep until 5:30 a.m. Refused toileting. Noisy, bouncing, cooperative with taking pills. Refused breakfast, but ate two Pop·Tarts.
	Looking in closet for clothes. Threw laundry hamper across room and threw himself on the floor. Loud noises but not understandable words. Tried to figure out if he was looking for something specific, but I couldn't figure out what he wanted.
	Finally got dressed but continued being noisy.
	Breakfast—good appetite, piercing screaming. To school bus.
	Teacher's note says irritable all day for no apparent reason.
	Enjoyed milk and cookies. Asked for second helping.
	Cooperated with outside activities. Took time to pet horse—smiling at her. Wanted to fetch with dog.
	Cued him to turn kitchen light on. Started screaming.
	Continued noise but cooperated with washing hands, changing placemats, setting table, peeling potatoes.
	Turned kitchen light off on his own. Quieter when we sat at the table to eat.
	Helped with clearing table, took bath, skin care, read *The Runaway Bunny* together, to bed with movie at 8:30 p.m.

home communication book from the teacher that you can refer to later.

- Calm periods where he cooperated well in whatever he was doing. Note what was going on before the calm period and what the activity was.

- Positive behaviors that you want to reinforce.

- If he was taking any new medications or experiencing any health situations.

- If any new foods were introduced.

- How much sleep he got.

- Any physical problems, such a virus or a toothache.
- Any change in normal schedule such as doctor's appointment, shopping, etc.

For now, it will work best if you start with just observing without trying to change anything.

In your journal, note activities and behaviors in enough detail to list what happened, but not in obsessive detail. When you are having a difficult time with your child or are extra busy you won't have time to worry about sentence structure, etc. Just list enough detail to help you remember what occurred. You want to see what worked well and what triggered some sort of negative response. Notice in particular what the circumstances or events were just before the incident you are writing about. For example, were you vacuuming or delayed on the telephone just before he behaved aggressively? The journal will help to catch patterns that bring on your child's positive or negative reactions. Also note how you handled the incident. Did you praise him for his good behavior or his positive performance of an activity? How did you deal with negative behavior, and what was the result? For example, did you calm him down when he showed aggressive behavior? How did you do that?

If you are out in the community, note any differences that occur just before a negative behavior. If you were in a store or restaurant that was noisy, did it affect his behavior? If you went to some place he was familiar with, did his behavior improve? Did a store clerk or a waiter make an extra effort to meet your child's needs? By noting the incident, eventually you may be able to plan community outings around some of those helpful people. For example, we know that when Billy Ray has to have blood work done he will be more comfortable with a certain lab technician who works only two evenings a week. We go on the nights Jeff is available whenever possible.

TRACKING BEHAVIOR

After a couple weeks of observing, review the journal. Pay attention to patterns of behavior or reactions to stimuli. For example, is she calmer if she does one activity before she does a different one? Does one activity seem to set her off every time? Remember that you are looking for behaviors you want to reinforce as well as those you want to modify later.

It helps to have a set of colored highlighting pens. You can highlight certain difficult behaviors in one color, calm or cooperative times in another, patterns that seem to emerge (for example, behavior following a night of good sleep or a certain activity), etc. As your journal gets thicker, it might be helpful to have those little "flags" you can buy in the office-supply stores. They come in two sizes, one narrow and one slightly wider so you can write a short comment. One end sticks to the area you want to find easily. The other end is colored. Marking a behavior you are tracking with one color every time it occurs and sticking a flag of the same color on that page makes finding the instances of that behavior quick and easy when you are trying to make a summary to share with the doctor.

With your journal in front of you, review positive behaviors you want to reinforce and those you would like to modify. Positive behaviors are anything that your child cooperates with and seems to enjoy and that you feel comfortable with. Examples may be a chore, a community outing, or a leisure activity at home that drew a positive response from your child. Reinforcing positive behavior gives your child increased confidence. That is a great starting point. While observing, try using the following questions as a guide and note your answers and other observations.

- What is the behavior you want to reinforce?

- Does he respond the same way to this activity every time?

- If he responds to the same activity positively one time and negatively another, ask yourself the following:

  - When he responded positively to _____ (activity), what was going on just before?

  - How did you communicate the activity to him when he responded positively?

  - Did you communicate the activity to him differently when he responded negatively to the activity?

  - What form of praise or reward did you give when he responded positively?

  - Did he respond positively the next time you tried the event?

Make a list of the behaviors you want to modify. There are blank forms to track behaviors on my website, www.parentingyourcomplexchild .com.

In the first column, "Description of Behavior," describe as completely as possible what occurs. If he throws something, list what was thrown and whether it was aimed at something or someone or just thrown aimlessly. Make the second column "How Often Does It Occur?" Note whether it is a single occurrence in the time you have been observing, happens daily, or occurs with some other frequency. Make the third column "Severity." List whether it was a mild, moderate, or major problem. Here are a few examples to help you determine the severity of a behavior:

Mild Behaviors:

- Throwing himself on the floor, refusing to move, but not hurting himself or others
- Some form of self-abuse or aggression that does not physically hurt himself or others
- A slap that does not hurt or cause a red mark
- Throwing a toy aimlessly (just throwing to be throwing, not in an attempt to break something)

Moderate Behaviors:

- Self-abuse or aggression that may hurt at the time but will cause no long-term injury
- A slap or other aggression that can be felt and may cause a red mark but no serious injury
- Minor property destruction

Severe Behaviors:

- Behavior that causes injury to self or others that usually requires medical treatment
- Behavior that causes severe property destruction, such as breaking something

Make the fourth column "What Triggers It." You may or may not know how to respond at this point. Look at each reoccurrence of the behavior. If you have made notes about what was going on just before the behavior, look to see if there was any reoccurrence of this circumstance. For example, maybe he screams every time the telephone rings or throws himself on the floor while trying to choose clothes. If the same behavior happens fairly often after similar events, something in that event is triggering the behavior. It may not be clear at first what about that event is the trigger, but you will have narrowed it down to an event.

SIFTING THROUGH THE DATA

After you have finished gleaning behavior data from your journal, choose one positive behavior that you want to reinforce. Look at the times he responded the most positively. Plan to create similar conditions to explore whether you get the same positive response.

Look over the list of behaviors you want to modify. Make note of questions you have and behaviors you want to observe more closely before you are ready to deal with them. For the next couple of weeks, while you are working to reinforce the positive behavior you have chosen, you can also observe the difficult behaviors from your list to understand them better. Perhaps the answers to some of the questions you noted will become apparent.

During a quiet time, gather the journal, the data you collected on positive and negative behaviors, and your notes on what a normal day is like now. Look at the positive and negative behaviors. Look at the sequence in his schedule. Is there something in the sequence (order) of his schedule that you think could be bothering him?

For example, take a look at the question about what your child asks first thing in the morning. If she is nonverbal, her behavior may demonstrate what she is interested in first thing. Is she trying to get dressed before using the toilet or eating breakfast, and is she resistant to the order in which you are trying to get her to do things? As you look at that, try to pick two or three things that you will have her do in sequence every morning and track her response for at least three days of doing it that way. I like to create simple forms to help me record Billy Ray's responses. You can print a blank form from www.parentingyourcomplexchild.com or just write your own in your journal or on blank paper.

List each of the three activities you are going to have her do in sequence. Leave space to list whether she was responsive to the activity and any alternative that was offered for lack of responsiveness to the activity.

If you get some inconsistency and are not sure that the change in sequence is helping, you might want to try it for another two or three days. If it is still not clear, take another look at the original sequence of activities and journal notes during that period. You may want to go back to the old sequence for a few days and note your child's response. If it is better than trying the new schedule sequence, don't be afraid to acknowledge the experiment was the wrong approach and try something else. Trial and error is necessary. The lack of success with a particular experiment just means to keep trying.

TAKE IT SLOW

As you are ready to try more experiments, do them slowly. It is less confusing for your child and less exhausting for you. We all want to "fix" our children immediately, but taking baby steps will help you clearly see what works and what doesn't work.

Pushing change too fast rarely works with any child, let alone a complex one. Consider how we often overreact, out of desire to help our child, if a professional makes a suggestion. When Billy Ray was in the hospital, for example, the psychiatric nurse said to get rid of everything stimulating in his bedroom at home. She recommended neutral solid colors such as medium blue rather than prints or bright colors. Acting on her suggestion, we stripped his room. We gave away all our Disney cartoon sheets with matching comforters and bought my son mellow bedding and curtains. When he came home from the hospital, his room was no longer home to him. His behavior was out of control, which may have been an indication that we made the change too rapidly. We ended up buying some items to make his room more like before and he relaxed. Later we tried to make these changes more gradually, and they helped.

Environment is a difficult thing to deal with, especially the environment in your child's bedroom. It is possible that having too many things in his bedroom stimulates him. This could be affecting his sleep or causing agitation. He may know exactly what he has in his room and resist having anything removed. Monitor how his room is arranged and how stimulating the colors are to him. Some children can handle action figures displayed on curtains, bedspreads, posters, and wallpaper, while others would be overly stimulated. If you feel your child is overly stimulated, try replacing items very gradually with more moderate items, such as those featuring soft colors without patterns. If you rearrange the furniture, do it a step or two at a time. If possible, involve your child in rearranging his own room. If you remove something, hide it rather than dispose of it, even if he has agreed to removing it. Retain it for a short time to ensure that he is not devastated by removing it. Whether he agreed to removal or not, he may not be able to tolerate losing the item right now. You have to restore it at least temporarily.

When looking at possible changes, start with simple things you notice. Here's an example of something we learned that made mealtime easier. Billy Ray was increasingly noisy at mealtimes shortly after we had moved into a new home. This continued for months. He would also throw the napkin holder or salt and pepper shakers. Mealtimes were less than pleasant.

My husband read that sometimes fluorescent lights give off a sound most of us don't hear, but some autistic children are agitated by it because of their sensitive hearing. Our new kitchen had a series of fluorescent lights—one of which was only a few feet from Billy Ray's chair at the dining room table. When we noted behaviors that occurred during meal times and what was happening before, during, and after the incident, we could see that the lights, the noise from the fan over the stove, or the running dishwasher agitated Billy Ray. If we used only the light over the dining table and the light over the stove—neither of which are fluorescent—and minimize other noises, it reduced his agitation during dinner.

Leave the more difficult behaviors to experiment with until you feel ready to deal with the temporary impact of making changes in your child's routine. Sometimes a child will behave negatively even if the change in routine is something he likes.

LEARNING ABOUT YOUR CHILD

We do much learning about our children by natural instinct. When Billy Ray became my son in 1984, there were not nearly as many books available for parents. It brought a smile to my face when I realized how many of the recommendations in recent books we had inadvertently followed because they seemed natural at the time.

For example, several professionals suggest floor time. Floor time is playing with your child or doing learning activities, usually sitting on the floor with her. It is great for bonding and getting to know what your child can do. We did a modification of that before I ever heard the term *floor time*.

At the time of Billy Ray's adoption, the commercial for the Sweet Pickles Bus learning program was constantly on the television and radio. The program included cards for various concepts and activities that went into a box that looked like a school bus. We ordered it and worked with Billy Ray a great deal on the various skills. We counted together and we knew he could count to fourteen, although he routinely mixed up the number six. Thus, when his preschool teacher stated that he could only count to two, we knew that was not accurate.

The Sweet Pickles activity cards came about every two weeks. We would work through them a few times at the table or on the floor. Then we used the skill from the cards in daily activities. We counted spoons as we put them in the dishwasher together, silverware to put on the table, items we were putting in the shopping cart when we were grocery shopping, etc. If the cards were teaching shapes, we talked about shapes of objects we were using in our regular activities. We named colors as we handled colored objects or sorted laundry.

If your child is receptive to learning skills while going about daily living, this adds other benefits to the floor time. You can make teaching life skills like playing so it is still pleasant for both of you. The child feels like he is helping, and you are able to get something done without sacrificing quality time with your child.

Depending on the age, functioning, and tendencies of your child, he may be able to participate in some tasks and not others. Think about things that you know he can do. Maybe he can pick up his toys independently. Make a note of these tasks and think about ways this skill might be applied to other tasks.

Learning about Billy Ray by doing things together was easier when he was younger. When Billy Ray changed dramatically at fourteen years old, we needed to start again. Floor time is a challenge with a fourteen-year-old who is not as interested in playing with toys, coloring, or doing learning exercises and has little attention span.

When we met my present husband, Billy Ray was very interested in Larry's horses. He loved to go to the barn to feed them and interact with them. After his personality changed, he made sudden movements and lots of noise, which upset the horses and created a dangerous situation for all. We told Billy Ray that he could not go into the barn unless he could stay calm and quiet. Medication did not control this behavior consistently, especially in the late afternoon when Billy Ray had the opportunity to be with the horses. We noted that motivation to feed his horses caused him to strive to control his behavior. He was able to feed them probably 90 to 95 percent of the time. I repeatedly told the psychiatrist and educational professionals that if we could figure out how to motivate him in other areas of his life the way feeding the horses motivated him, his life would be better. This idea seemed to be insignificant to everyone but me.

By the way, it is never too soon to watch for natural talents and interests, which might work into something meaningful in your child's adult life. Be observant as you are developing his present situation. Think about ways to use talents that could lead to employment or at least a meaningful activity for your child. Our former neighbor, a 4-H leader, suggested that because Billy Ray enjoys feeding horses and even scooping horse poop in our barn, he may be able to make a career out of it. She said farmers have difficulty finding anyone willing to do that. Sometimes busy professionals have horses and would love to have someone like Billy Ray come and feed their animals and clean the barn.

RECOGNIZING PATTERNS

It made little sense that he could do so many things but was no longer interested in participating. School was not working well. I made a list of all the things he could do but refused to do, the things he would occasionally agree to do, and the things he did often. Patterns began to emerge from those lists; the things he frequently agreed to do were active tasks, and they all followed a consistent schedule. For example, walking to the barn, giving the horses grain, and pushing the hay cart out to throw hay into the pasture for them was not only an active task—he knew when to expect the activity every day.

Try involving your child in as many routine activities as you can, whether he has done them before or not. As you keep track of what your child is interested in doing versus what he refuses to try, you can compare the types of activities, the time of the day, etc., and see if patterns emerge. Ask yourself if there is something distasteful or irritating for him in things he refuses to do. What motivates him in activities he enjoys? Be sure to include activities in the home and community activities. It will surprise you what you are learning about your child.

Sometimes it is not the activity itself that your child resists, but the order of activities. He may be confused about what you expect of him. As you spend time with your child, paying extra attention to his responses, these details may be more obvious. If not, experiment until it seems clear.

Other refusal-to-participate incidents may occur because you are not able to communicate to your child the way he needs to receive information about the intended activity or the behavior.

COMMUNICATING WITH YOUR CHILD

As you glean information about your child, experiment with different methods of communicating with him, and note his reactions in various trials. You do not have to create full-blown systems for these trials. Here are a couple of things to try:

1. Cut out a few pictures from a magazine or even a coloring book that are close to an activity or task you want to try with your child. Show him one of the pictures and tell him that you are going to do that activity. Another time, try a different picture and note his response. By doing this several times, you will see more clearly if it is the communication method he is responding to or failing to respond to, as opposed to being interested or not interested in the activity itself.

2. If you have an appointment coming up that is not something he does often or he is resistant to, draw pictures of the steps involved and write a short description of each step. You certainly do not need to

make as this as complicated as the digital-picture stories discussed earlier, especially in this experimental phase. Keep it as brief as possible but answer these questions: What is he going to do? Where is he going? Why he is going to do it? What is expected of him? An example of the Feeding the Horse visual is in appendix figure 2, and more can be viewed on my website: www.parentingyourcomplexchild.com.

Note the responses you get to these approaches. They will help when deciding on communication methods and daily schedules for your child.

In addition to experimenting with how you communicate with your child, experiment with ways he can communicate with you better. When Billy Ray is unresponsive verbally to a question or request, we have discovered that we can sometimes give him an action to demonstrate his answer. For example, if he is not responding verbally we can say, "If you want to go feed your horses, put your barn shoes on." If he starts putting on his shoes, we know that he wants to do the activity but can't respond verbally at that moment. For things that we don't have activities to demonstrate, we have a communication book with pictures of people, places, and things he might be trying to request but can't verbalize at that time. When he seems frustrated, we can give him the notebook and say, "Show me what you want." We do not need to use it often, but there are times it reduces aggressive behaviors significantly.

HANDLING POWER STRUGGLES

Power struggles come in many forms with complex children. Some of these arise because of their overly logical or illogical thought processing. We can't avoid power struggles altogether, but they can be minimized, especially with preventive approaches.

One of the hardest things to accept was that Billy Ray could no longer be reasoned with. It took years after his change to realize that his seemingly stubborn and defiant behavior was often his inability to be logical. This may be difficult for you to evaluate in your child, too. Make an effort to watch his responses to "no" or your explanations of why he cannot have what he wants. Keep track of several such events so you can compare later.

Compare his reactions to negative responses from you, such as "no" or "I don't know." Does he seem angrier about not getting what he wants, or is he genuinely unable to understand? Once a child is focused so strongly on a need or want, he can't focus on anything else. If possible, deal with the issue immediately upon his request or question. Try to avoid saying no. Giving him a detailed explanation of why he can't have what he wants is generally unsuccessful. Try using phrases like "I would rather we do _____" or "It would be better to _____." If he fails to accept that, you have to evaluate the importance of your response. Picking your battles is necessary. If he wants something that is harmful to him, stand your ground. If it is not a big deal, state your position without a firm refusal and be prepared to give in rather than endure the power struggle.

Take some time to think about frequent power struggles when you are not in the middle of one. Are there ways that you can avoid them? If it is a timing issue, make sure that he knows he will do the desired activity at a specific time so he is secure in being able to do it at the appropriate time. If a power struggle is caused by him seeing a desirable item, it may help to make such items less visible.

Pay attention to his sense of time and order of events and keep notes. Billy Ray doesn't tell time by the clock, but he knows when a staff member is late by even five minutes. He has no concept of time for appointments, etc. He is not able to accept that if he does not cooperate with getting ready by a certain time, it will be too late for the activity. For example, if he does not have a certain item of clothing available, he refuses to go to an appointment or activity until we wash it, even if we have planned what he is going to wear the night before. Maybe he just wants to ensure it is in his closet. He is not able to understand that meetings, appointments, or church services don't wait for him to do what he is insisting on doing first. If there is something that your child gets stuck about consistently, make notes about it along with any ideas to avoid the problem that come to mind. If you do not have resolutions now, they may occur to you when you review the journal later.

In the example about clothing, we are able to avoid that problem if we put all of Billy Ray's laundry in the washing machine before he goes to bed at night. If I put it in the dryer and return it to his closet by the time he wakes up in the morning, we have eliminated a big part of the struggle to get him out the door. As you look at problem areas, apply that kind of thinking to the problems you face. Consider if there is some preventive action that will reduce the incidence of friction.

GETTING ALONG WITH YOUR CHILD

In addition to getting to know your child better, it is necessary to see how she fits within your family. Personality conflicts with your complex child happen just like with other members of the family. You may love her and still not like everything about her. Whether you realize it or not, she may feel the same way about you. The things she does that irritate you are easier for you to see. She may not be able to communicate to you that something you do is driving her crazy.

In his book, *Special Children, Challenged Parents* (Brookes Publishing Company, 2001), Robert A. Naseef, Ph.D., talks about temperamental mismatch between parent and child. This is where the nature and characteristics of the parent and child are different. That describes my relationship with Billy Ray following the day he had the seizures. I loved him and was just as committed to him as ever, but I had difficulty with his new personality.

Before he changed, we were well suited. I enjoyed taking him everywhere possible just to be together, and I loved talking with him or rocking him. He loved being nurtured and cuddled. He was generally a quiet child who could be content to play with his toys in his bedroom across the hall from the bathroom while I took a bubble bath. We enjoyed lots of together time, but he could be trusted to give me space, too.

Billy Ray was so polite and socially acceptable that I was able to build my fiduciary business around having him with me whenever school holidays or vacations occurred. My elderly clients adored seeing him and he them. He went to law offices and sat quietly like a little man, drawing on a legal pad with his markers while I took care of my business. In the space I rented next door to my actual office was a multipurpose room with a table where I held meetings with attorneys and/or clients' families. This "conference room" also served as Billy Ray's "office" with his own desk, books, colors, television, video player, and movies.

Noise, even the fan on the fireplace or air conditioner, bothers me.

What I need first thing in the morning is quiet with my coffee and lots of time to wake up. Billy Ray used to wake up smiling and would sit at the table eating his breakfast quietly while I drank my coffee and woke up fully. He was fine with having the television news on low so we could catch up on local events.

Since his life-changing event, he generally wakes up yelling so loudly that I have three times taken him to the ear, nose, and throat specialist to be sure he hasn't damaged his throat. Most of his verbalizations are not requests that I can fulfill. It is just noise, not all of it understandable. In addition, he routinely bounces up and down or runs around the house as though he were doing track. Given his tendency to pick up objects and throw them before his medication has had time to take effect, it is best to stay in close proximity to him. This means sometimes following him in his tour from one end of the house to the other while trying to get him to the kitchen so we can get his juice and medication. It also means that sometimes I have to juggle juice and the little bowl we put his pills in with one hand while trying to put my other hand on his shoulder to catch his attention to stop bouncing long enough to take his medication.

How do you reconcile so much temperamental difference? The first six months, I tolerated my son because his pediatrician said that in most cases children come back to what was normal for them within three to six months following their seizures. I kept expecting the old Billy Ray to come back. After that, I began to realize that this was the same little boy I loved. I tried to remember things that were special between us before the change and somehow adapt as many as possible to the present Billy Ray. But I often have to simply accept situations that are uncomfortable for me. For example, doing busy activities with him to try to keep him focused first thing in the morning until his medications can kick in is quite the opposite of the quiet, slow-moving morning I crave.

When the problem is that your child has issues that are hard for you to accept, it is easier to adapt than if you have issues that bother your child. We have both. Long before Billy Ray became my son, I was a disorganized housekeeper and had problems with clutter. That worked well for Billy Ray in the beginning because I am a people person and he was my priority. The clutter did not appear to bother him.

After he developed autistic-like symptoms, clutter bothered him. He can accept a pile of magazines or some project I have started and not finished on the end table by my chair, but some new clutter will bother him until he throws it. This is especially true if the clutter collects on our dining room table, which is a constant battle between us.

Our issues in this area are very complicated. My favorite author on the topic, Sandra Felton, who wrote *The Messies Manual* (Fleming H. Revell, 1983) and many other books, says that messy people are not lazy, they are really perfectionists. They are trying to do too many things at once and end up with unfinished projects all over the house, creating chaos. Billy Ray contributes to the chaos; I can rarely finish a project because of his interruptions for care and supervision. It is often necessary to do things on the run to keep up with him.

You have only so much time and energy to deal with issues like this. Your child certainly adds to the problem. It is easy to resent this. Try to avoid getting stuck in that. Involve your child in the solution to the highest degree possible. Ask him to help you pick up things and put them away. Explain that you will work together to make things more pleasant for everyone.

Another area that might be a mismatch is your child's sleep habits and your own. Maybe he has major sleep issues and will stay in his room only if you are in there with him. Adapt what works for both of you. If that means that you are so exhausted you put a sleeping bag in the door and catnap, do it. Maybe you can trust him to stay in bed while you relax in a recliner next to his bed. During this phase, experiment a bit with bedtimes and methods until you discover what works. Make notes for use in creating a schedule later.

Children with disabilities are so often referred to as having special needs and their parents as saints, it can be hard to think about our mutual humanness. Whatever your child's situation developmentally or physically, you have to see him first and his disabilities second. You need to see yourself with strengths and weaknesses like everyone else. Don't put unrealistic expectations on either your child or yourself.

With time and practice your own insight may surprise you. You will know your child even better than you think you do now. As you do this, you will know what is most important for her and for you. Accept that you will make mistakes, and start again when you do. Don't be afraid to try again. Be open with your child. Tell her that what you tried seemed to make her uncomfortable, so you are going to try something new. She may see this whole experiment as a game and love playing it.

WORKING WITH THE IEP TEAM

Your interpretation about what is best for your child and the interpretations of others may be different. Sometimes you have to create systems at home to show others what your child needs. In addition, knowing your child better will help you to get support for educational and other services that you feel are appropriate. When you can demonstrate what your child is capable of doing and better ways of relating to her, appropriate goals and plans generally follow.

Before you get too far into observing your child, it is a good idea to sit down with her IEP. Look at the level of performance the IEP states she has achieved and the goals set for her. It is helpful to have them in mind when you are working with your child. It is entirely possible you will see results that are different from what the IEP demonstrates.

It is easier and cheaper for schools and other programs to try to push a child into existing systems than create one that works for an individual child. We have experienced that with Billy Ray repeatedly. He is a child who needs to be up and moving around a significant portion of his day. He is not happy to sit around a table for group activities. Observe your child in various activities at home and at school. Make notes about what things seem to interest her. In addition, track what brings about a negative reaction. The chances are strong that your child will perform best with you. You will be able to share the information on performance in certain areas at home, but only if you make the time to find out what she can do.

If you have access to a camcorder and a tripod (sometimes you can borrow one from your county developmental disabilities office or other organizations that support disabled persons), turning it on and just letting it record your child's activities is very helpful. When you look at the video later, you may well catch more than you saw when you were busy interacting with your child. Perhaps you can see another way of approaching the activity or communicating with your child.

Once she starts to do well, sharing these videos with the IEP team is a good way to show how your approaches work better than approaches they might be trying at school.

9

Two Essential Words: *Communicate* and *Adapt*

AT TIMES when nothing seems to be working at home or school, it is hard to see the butterfly among the weeds that seem to prevent your child and you from walking the garden path. Maybe you really like his teacher and feel she really cares for your child, but you do not understand why he is not cooperating in school. Maybe the therapist recommends programs that seem to work well for other children, but the same program is uninspiring to your child.

We want to do the right thing for our children. It seems important to try methods exactly as suggested, but we are disappointed when they do not help. A perfectly good approach for other children may need to be modified for your child.

If you don't remember anything else about this book, I hope you will remember these two critical words: *communicate* and *adapt*. Keep repeating in your mind "communicate, adapt, and communicate." First, adjust your communication with your child to learn everything she can teach you about her needs. Armed with lessons learned from observing and communicating with your child, you can adapt her activities and environment to what is most comfortable for her. Finally, communicate to her community and to those involved in her care and education what your child can do and what she needs to thrive in her world.

HELPING BILLY RAY COMMUNICATE

I keep talking about visuals for Billy Ray because they have transformed his life. They are a classic example of the message of this chapter: Learn from your child through communication and then do what works for your child—whether it is using visuals or something else you adapt to your child.

Billy Ray's articulation was not a major problem for me when he was younger. Others had a lot of difficulty understanding him. (Dr. Ron used to say, "If only everyone could understand you through your mother's ears and eyes.") During an evaluation at two years old, we were told that he was primed and ready for speech therapy, but the waiting list to see our HMO's speech specialists was long. If we waited for that, he might not be as motivated, so we elected to get private speech therapy through a local hospital. Speaking clearly was an effort for him—mostly because of his thick tongue, which sometimes accompanies Down syndrome—but he worked very hard with the therapist.

His use of speech slowed following his medication reaction in puberty. He does not always articulate as well as he once did. However, the most noticeable change is in his ability to "get it out." When you ask him a question or give him a request, he may answer immediately, but other times you need to allow enough time for him to respond. To repeatedly make demands on him without allowing him time to incorporate what you have said and respond frustrates him to the point of occasionally causing aggression. Then there are times he may not be able to respond verbally at all. At those times when he cannot get the words out, we have learned that we can cue him to demonstrate by some action. For example, if we are asking him if he wants to go somewhere, but he is unresponsive, we might say, "If you want to go, get your coat on." Many times, he is much more able to respond with action than speech.

Sometimes it is like he does not hear at all. He is often in his own world and not hearing a thing that is said to him. I discovered that if I give him a picture symbol, he is able to understand more quickly what I am trying to communicate to him.

I described earlier how I got frustrated with the software I was using, because I was able to find symbols for sex and swear words but not for common activities and roles. A friend loaned me a digital camera she seldom used. It was apparent immediately that Billy Ray responded to digital-picture schedules better than to the software symbols.

The case manager had also purchased a program called Social Stories™ by Carol Gray for us. Ms. Gray shares a great deal of helpful information on the videotapes in her program about how to communicate with autistic children. Additionally, my husband, Larry, found the Center for the Study of Autism website (www.autism.com), which is an affiliate of the Autism Research Institute. Larry printed out article after article from that site, especially those written by Temple Grandin.

The understanding that I gleaned about how autistic children receive information made such a difference in my ability to understand my son. We also read many of Dr. Grandin's books and those of others. Billy Ray functioned on a lower level than most of the books addressed. I can't say that I came away with specific procedures for my child, but I really wasn't looking for that. I was more desperate to communicate with my son. The most important thing I learned is how to understand and communicate with my son on his level. Armed with this, I could then work to adapt approaches to a low-functioning individual like my son.

I was taking pictures of each step in an activity and writing text about each step. Some activities took more than one page. The consultant assisting us at the time would say, "You will lose his interest if they are too long." So I shortened them and tried to "do it right," but discovered Billy Ray responded only to my detailed visuals that contained real pictures. Again, you must adapt to your child's needs and responses, not someone else's ideas.

Eventually we got a scanner and Larry scanned everything, even old Polaroid pictures. We wrote stories about various events in Billy Ray's life, such as the story of his adoption. These were called *Billy Ray's Stories*. He loved having his stories read to him and seeing pictures of himself doing the activities. You have to do what works for your child, period.

The activity visuals I created helped Billy Ray to understand each step in an activity. They served the additional purpose of reminding care-giving staff of the order in which the activities are done. Billy Ray seems to require things to be in the same sequence (order) to avoid confusion and agitation. If he is able to have this consistency between caregivers and family, it helps prevent behavior caused by frustration or confusion.

ADAPTING TO YOUR INDIVIDUAL CHILD

This communication system was what it took to jump-start Billy Ray. Now I knew how to approach projects and create a picture schedule that would be more interesting to him. Your child may need a different proce-dure. Many times professionals' ideas get you thinking. You may be able to revise their ideas into a workable approach for your child. Don't con-sider any program or procedure to be too sacred to alter; adapt it to what your child is able to use.

Communicating with your child is the first step to being able to adapt to him. Sometimes that will be through talking to him. Sometimes it means watching his responses to changes in his routine or environment. I missed being able to just ask Billy Ray what was going on or what he wanted. I could not always understand his responses when he was little, but he was able to convey the message somehow because he wanted to be understood as much as I wanted to understand. After the onset of autistic-like symptoms, communication between us literally ceased. A two-way conversation for us now rarely happens. Eventually I began to be able to read his behavior more than his words. That is not to say that I understand his entire behavior even now. However, if I step back and think about how he responded to an activity or request, I can often un-derstand what was going on with him.

Night after sleepless night, I sat in Billy Ray's room (so he would stay in his room) and thought about what had worked in his life and what had not. I thought about the approaches used by others as well as myself.

I thought about his most successful year, as I described in chapter 6.

His teacher, Connie, took my information about what he was able to do and used her creativity to help him achieve so much during that partial year. I learned so much from her. Later I tried to apply the same techniques to see if we could get back at least some of that confident, high-functioning Billy Ray.

Even minor adaptations, such as which activity he will do first or communicating with him using visual cues, can sometimes make major differences in a child's ability to function comfortably and perform at higher levels than before.

As a parent, you have always known your child best. Some of what you see may be tainted because it becomes routine. Taking the time for closer observation can reveal things you did not realize, even though your child may have experienced it every day for years. Medical, educational, or social-work professionals see your child as he is in a professional environment. You see how he behaves in the supermarket as opposed to a doctor's office or classroom. You see what can be accomplished when he knows what is expected of him and what he will do next. It takes time to understand how to adapt environments, activities, and schedules to your child. Give your child and yourself as much time as you need.

The special-needs community has many experts who have helped untold children to have better lives. Their methods may work wonderfully for many children, but they may not work for your child exactly as designed. By adapting those methods or parts of those methods to what works best for your individual child, sometimes programs that fail to help exactly as recommended will become useful.

COMMUNICATING WITH PROFESSIONALS

Communicating doesn't stop with your child. As you learn what she needs and adapt her environment to fit her needs, you can communicate to various professionals what she can do and how she can function best.

It was difficult for medical, educational, and social-work professionals to believe my claims of what Billy Ray could do. The Billy Ray they saw threw himself on the floor, refused to sit in his chair for table activities, and created havoc in many settings. Thus, when I said, "If only we could figure out how to bring this motivation to control his behavior into the rest of his life, he'd be happier and need less medication," the professionals could not picture what I was describing. Later, I brought the activity visuals to an IEP meeting. The visuals showed Billy Ray actively involved in feeding his horse (see appendix figure 2). I could see the surprise on the faces of several team members. Some of them commented on how he looked substantially independent while performing those tasks. Others admitted they would not have believed he could do that level of activity had they not seen the pictures. Two professionals made appointments to come to our home to observe some of the other things he could do. Unfortunately, sometimes we have to prove our children to others.

On the other hand, professionals can communicate important messages to you that you might not realize on your own. Our developmental pediatrician, Dr. O'Brien, taught me about risk taking. When Billy Ray was little, I was worried because he would eat crayons. Dr. O'Brien said that the risk of harm from eating crayons was less than the cost of not learning the developmental skill. We also talked about the risk of Billy Ray having a dog, because he was so rough with her. She explained that the main risk of a dog bite was infection, but if treated immediately that was unlikely to be a major problem. The doctor said that the benefit he got from the dog far exceeded the risk. Dr. O'Brien taught me to weigh the risks against the benefits when establishing an environment for my son—another side of learning to adapt.

ADAPTING YOUR FAMILY ENVIRONMENT

You should not overlook the importance of adaptations that make life tolerable for you and the family unit as a whole. As I wrote in the caregiver manual I prepared for our in-home staff, "Although our home is effectively a treatment center for one child, it is still the family home of all three of us." Your home can feel like an institution because of the environment you must create for your child. That can wear on some of us, while others tolerate it better. Think about what you need to feel comfortable in your own home. Give yourself permission to refuse some things that others recommend for your child if those things feel too invasive for you.

In our prior home, the only bathtub was in the master bathroom.

Billy Ray is terrified of showers. When caregiving staff assisted with his bath, it was necessary for them to come into what should be private space for my husband and me. Additionally it meant modifying what we could have in our private bathroom and that a grab bar had to be put on our tub to help Billy Ray get in and out. We felt that our privacy was somewhat invaded by that, but dealt with it out of necessity.

During the period we were in that house, the consultant and one of the school specialists both suggested that I post the activity visuals I had made about his bath in our bathroom so that he could see them when he was taking his bath. I could see the benefit to Billy Ray, but I bristled at giving up any more. We had removed trinkets that I loved from the master suite because they would be attractive nuisances tempting him to throw them. To post his visuals in there too was like asking us to turn even our private space into an institutional environment. This was another turning point of sorts.

The first time it was suggested, I felt guilty at my own reaction. Eventually it became clear that in order for a sense of home to be maintained for all the family members, there need to be adaptations for everyone. If that means some minor sacrifice on the part of a disabled child, it just has to be.

Dr. O'Brien, the developmental pediatrician, encouraged me to take care of myself so that I could take care of Billy Ray. When I married Larry, he had the grandchildren I had always dreamed of having. After Billy Ray changed dramatically, some of the grandkids were frightened of him. I talked to Dr. O'Brien about how to explain him to his stepnieces and nephews. She gave me some helpful information on how to educate the grandkids; however, she gave me some surprising advice as well. She said that Larry and I needed the time with the grandchildren to be healthy and happy. The grandchildren needed us too. She said that if it was necessary to use the as-needed medication to help Billy Ray take a nap once in a while so we could visit with the grandchildren, we should do that. She said that it would not hurt him to have an extra nap and it would "refill your bucket so you have something left to give to him."

Over the years, I have often used that advice to adapt our lives and environments for all of us. For example, trinkets that are special gifts from others are put away. We buy Wal-Mart or dime-store trinkets that are not major losses if Billy Ray breaks them. He will almost always throw pretty salt and pepper shakers and napkin holders, so I bought plastic shakers and put them and the dinner napkins into one of the lovely baskets my mother-in-law gives me with various holiday gifts in them. If Billy Ray throws it, the only damage is some wasted napkins.

Again, adapting is the key. Although Billy Ray may leave them alone for months or even years, eventually, he will be compelled to throw a trinket. I can enjoy the cheap treasures and not have to worry about Billy Ray breaking the good trinkets. Because the cheap trinkets are made of plastic, there is no risk of Billy Ray picking up broken glass to play with it or put it in his mouth. It is important that you take time to adapt for yourselves as well as for your child. The old saying that you can't serve from an empty bucket is really true. Your child drains you regularly and is not able to give back as much as he takes. Your giving will run out if you don't do things to make you feel good about your life no matter how small they might be.

10

CREATING A LIFE THAT WORKS FOR YOUR CHILD AND YOUR FAMILY

IN CHAPTER 4, "Feeling Misunderstood," I discussed how easy it sometimes may seem to just give up. Drawing your complex child and your family into an isolated existence, going out only when necessary, may be a path of least resistance. Other people's reactions to your child are hard to cope with. Fighting with the school district or other agencies to get appropriate programs can feel like more frustration than it is worth.

Every member of the family has needs. Resentments occur when the complex child always takes priority. This is difficult to reconcile. In a single-parent household with only a complex child, you simply cannot leave your child unattended in order to do something you really need to do for yourself if his tendency is to hurt himself or destroy the house. Where there are two parents, trading time with the child helps one parent to get some of his or her individual needs met. Unfortunately, there is little time for each other. Even having a conversation is difficult when one of you must chase the child or he is so noisy you cannot hear each other speak. If there are sleep problems with the child, chances are both parents never make it to their own bed on the same night.

Where there are siblings, it is difficult to spend needed time with the other children because of care needs, interruptions, or behaviors of your complex child. Complex children require more attention than other family members. Realistically that will probably not change. Creating more predictability for the complex child enables the rest of the family to have a better life too.

GETTING YOUR CHILD MORE FOCUSED

When your complex child is out of focus or confused about his life, the idea of taking on the additional activities that *Parenting Your Complex Child* suggests might seem too much. It may be hard to see how you can make the extra effort and what good it will do your child. Your child's behavior when his life does not work for him takes a lot of time and energy. Sometimes changing a few things at home makes all the difference in the functioning of your child, which in turn affects the entire family.

You and your family would probably benefit greatly from some in-home help obtained through your local agencies. If your family can endure it, I recommend you work on getting your child more focused and at least started on a comfortable schedule before getting more help. If you bring in outside helpers who are unfamiliar with your child, they may not maintain the routine you are trying to get your child used to. That can disrupt the process for a while.

It will take more work with him in the beginning, but it will reduce the work later when you have schedules and other approaches working better for him. If you use some of the various kinds of visuals and other documentation, you will be able to use help provided by local agencies, volunteers from your church, and your family or friends more effectively.

When they are with your child, they will be more prepared to take care of him because they have visual or written instructions. Then it will be less stressful for you to leave him with someone, whether it is to go to work or for some other event.

Start with your complex child's schedule first. Behavior that is caused by frustration or confusion at not knowing what is expected of her and what she is going to do will disrupt her environment until you provide her with the information and consistency she needs. The more stable her schedule, the less likely these behaviors will affect the family. This allows opportunities for other people's needs to be met.

This is not to say you will get no behavior issues. Behaviors are caused by many things. Here I am specifically talking about behaviors expressing confusion or frustration. I believe this is a major factor for many children, but again each child is an individual. You will know best what triggers certain behaviors in your child, especially after spending time being extra observant.

In survival mode, the quality of your child's life and that of the rest of the family is not something you spend lots of time thinking about. You are just trying to get through each day and hoping for things like a few hours of sleep.

CONSIDER YOUR CHILD'S POINT OF VIEW

Step back in your mind's eye and try to look at things from your child's perspective if you can. It is hard enough to just find school programs or activities at home or in the community for a complex child. We do not always think about having enough challenges for our children. If she responds to her activities with anger or refusal to cooperate, we cannot understand why.

When your child is constantly agitated and refuses to cooperate throughout much of her day, it is helpful to try to put yourself into her life as much as possible. Then think about the times that you were irritable and unhappy with your life. Maybe it was as simple as hating your haircut or clothing. It could have been a supervisor or a teacher who drove you crazy. You may have had a job you hated. Maybe it was a class that was too hard or too boring. The list of potential causes could go on and on. Imagine that you were not able to understand what was irritating you and/or you were unable to communicate it to others in a way that would bring change. The frustration would continually grow. Perhaps that is exactly the situation your complex child is in.

When we were teenagers most of us said to our parents, "I'm not a baby." We hated being treated as a young child when we had matured beyond that level. Your child may not communicate it to you, but may well experience some of that same frustration.

It is much easier for us to do everything for our children than to be patient long enough to allow them to do as much as they can for themselves. When we started having caregivers help in the home, I saw this tendency in them before I saw it in myself. In the case of a disabled child, some of that is out of a desire to take care of the child and protect him. His self-worth can be affected by not being allowed to do as much as possible for himself. It is faster and easier to put a movie on for your child and do household tasks yourself. The messages this conveys to a child are:

- He is not capable of doing anything.
- It is everyone else's job to take care of him.
- He is a bother to the rest of the family.

Each of us has a job in life. A very young child shows pride in his or her accomplishments. Disabled children have to work harder sometimes, but they need that sense of accomplishment just as anyone else does. Being allowed to participate in his own life and that of his family is just as important to a disabled child.

I find myself repeatedly reminding caregivers that they should not tell Billy Ray, "Help me make your bed." It is his bed. Making his bed is his job. The cue verbally and visually, if necessary, is, "It is time to make your bed. If you need help, I am here." He may need help to accomplish this if it is time to change sheets, and it may not be perfect but it's his bed and his job. Our confidence or lack thereof in a child says much to him about his value as a person.

Success will not be a slam dunk for your child no matter at what level he functions. He will need confidence in himself, whether it is to function in a group-home setting, in an apartment program with some degree of independence, or in a college dorm. By giving him the sense that he can do things as young as possible, you build into him the desire to be as independent as possible.

Think about your child's life. As you put yourself into his life experience in your mind's eye, think about things that would irritate you. This may be helpful in finding part of the cause for his agitation. You can experiment with adapting areas of his life that you have identified as potential irritants.

Consider your child's reactions to different settings. Have you observed some task or activity that he appears to enjoy doing and that motivates him to control his behavior? If he responds negatively to certain tasks or activities, ask yourself what about that setting might bother him.

If something comes to mind that you think may be irritating your child, describe the situation in as much detail as you can in the journal. Read over what you have written, then put it away until tomorrow. Think about the potential irritant overnight. Then reread your notes. Sometimes the extra time to think about a problem area is what you need to come up with solutions.

Find a time when you can be alone with your child in a sort of quality minute. Take a trip to a drive-through for an ice cream, or sit on the floor and play with the dog together. Tell him you can see that he is bothered by something. Tell him that together you can make things better. Ask if him there is something you can do. If he is able to verbalize, give him lots of time to respond. If you have some idea of one or two things that might be bothering him, you might just ask. He may or may not be able to respond, but it is worth a try. If he is nonverbal, tell him that you are going to try to find out what is bothering him. Ask him to show you in any way that he can what is bothering him. Sometimes the response will amaze you. Other times there may be a sense of peace that he at least knows you care. If nothing comes of it, you will still open communication lines a little more. It helps him to feel like a part of the solution.

CREATING A WORKABLE SCHEDULE

Review the journal notes and forms you have been keeping from our discussion in chapter 8. As you do, ask yourself the following questions and make notes of what you find:

- Is there a pattern in how she wakes up in the morning that affects her behavior throughout the day? For example, is she too hyper to eat first thing in the morning, so that it takes too long to take medication that she must have with food? When Billy Ray was in that situation, I used to take his pills and a can of strawberry Boost (a nutritional supplement) and maybe a small sweet roll or some crackers that he likes into his room the minute he was awake. We no longer have that issue, but now the first question is, "Where we going?" and his behavior will be wild until we answer that question verbally many times and go over his picture schedule. He is then willing to do the things he needs to do to start his day. For your child, there might be something else preying on her mind. Try to think of an approach to resolve that particular issue.

- Are there any patterns in what sets off her negative behaviors, refusals to do certain activities, or "getting stuck"? If so, what can you do to avoid that situation or make it smoother? One example from Billy Ray is that he obsesses about his clothes. He often wants the clothes he wore yesterday—even if it is only to know that they are hanging in his closet. By having him put his laundry in the washer before he goes to bed, we solve two problems: (1) he is willing to get into sweats or pajamas instead of sleeping in his clothes (a battle we had for a while); and (2) the morning agitation and behavior problems because he can't wear dirty clothes are lessened—all of his clothes will be hanging in the closet.

- Are there predictable negative behaviors? If so, what can you do to avoid them? For example, if you know certain objects are likely to give her impulse-control issues, remove them or hide them, if possible. If events create the behaviors, will scheduling changes help, or can the activity be avoided?

- How does she receive communication best? Based on your experimentation and notes in your journal, does she respond to picture cues better on occasion? Would it help to create symbols, a picture schedule, or a written schedule she could check off when she is finished? Would writing out activity visuals for her to read or to be read to her, explaining an activity, be something she would respond to? If you have not experimented with this yet, it is worth trying.

- Based on your lists of skills and preferred activities, what activities would be best for her schedule?

Starting with one time period instead of the entire day is probably best. If your child is in school or a day program, you could work out a schedule for before or after school as a starting point. Make a draft schedule of the activities you want your child to do and in what order.

It is important to take a look at how flexible your child is able to be. For example, if Mom assists with the bath, she does things one way. If Dad assists with the bath, he may do it another way. Some children can go with the flow in terms of order. Others need absolute consistency in terms of sequence (order) of activities and steps within each activity. You can test this by observing the difference in your child when you take activities out of order or change the steps within an activity, as opposed to doing it the same way each time.

I will go into written instructions more in chapter 15, "Hiring, Training, and Supervising Caregivers," but for now here's a brief example of how important it can be for some children that the steps in an activity be done in consistent sequence by everyone involved in their care.

Despite my written and verbal instructions, a caregiving assistant changed the sequence of when Billy Ray would put on his undershirt following his bath and skin care. She would bathe him weekdays using the sequence that she had modified. I would bathe him on the weekend using the former sequence of steps. He was agitated three weekends in a row. One weekend he punched me on my shoulder out of his confusion. I could not understand it.

I asked the assistant if she was having any problems or if he was agitated for her. She related no problems. Then one day the consultant was present at a meeting with the assistant and me. The assistant announced that she had modified the sequence of when he put his undershirt on and that he seemed more comfortable with that. The reason he was agitated on the weekends was that I was not following the sequence she was following during the week. He knew what to expect during the five days she was working with him and was confused when I changed that. Her change was actually an improvement over the sequence we were using. The problem was she did not choose to communicate it with me so that we did it the same way on weekends. Consistency of routines is important for some complex children.

When Billy Ray was little, the neurologist told me that most young children get restless or active when their schedules are changed. He said when you change the routine for a developmentally disabled child, it is like taking him to a foreign country where he doesn't speak the language. Billy Ray basically needs to know every detail of what he is supposed to do to be comfortable.

If consistency is very important to your child, decide on a procedure that you and everyone involved with him are able to be consistent with and your child is the most likely to accept. Being detailed on procedures, so that you actually do things in the sequence you decide on, will help you to remember the exact procedure the next day and it will be available to alternate caregivers working with your child. Consider backup plans for activities where you think there might be refusal on your child's part.

The schedule you create has to work for you too. If it creates problems for you, inconsistency may be a problem that will affect your child's progress. Obviously, you want things to be the best for your child, but you also are a part of the plan.

CHOOSING A SCHEDULE FORMAT

Before presenting a new schedule to your child, decide in what format the schedule will be best prepared for your child to understand. Some children would be fine with a printed calendar much like a planner page you might use for yourself. You can get different types of sheets like that in the office supply store, get calendar software for your computer, or draw your own templates.

According to Temple Grandin (*Thinking in Pictures*, Vintage Books, 1995) many persons with autism, including herself, are visual thinkers. That is, they actually think in pictures. If your child responds more to pictures, a picture schedule of some sort may be better for him than verbal or written cues.

If you decide that your child will respond best to some sort of visual, take time to create them before you introduce a new schedule to your child. If you are not able to make them, you can generally get help through the school or your county or state developmental disabilities program. Sometimes they will make some visuals for you or have equipment available for parents to use.

It is easier if you can make at least some of your own schedules and/or visuals at home. You can make them as simple or as involved as you desire. Some consultants use Polaroid pictures and place them in the plastic notebook inserts made for storing floppy computer disks. You can get those in office supply stores. The advantage to taking Polaroids is that they are available immediately. You might even purchase a Polaroid camera very cheaply in a thrift store to get you started.

I started out with schedules using symbol software on the computer. I put the symbol for an activity on the left side and wrote the name of the activity on the right of the sheet. They were on my computer, but they had to be edited and reprinted every time Billy Ray had an appointment. I put them in "write-on" page protectors so we could check off items without having to reprint everyday. The idea of checking them off was abandoned eventually, when Billy Ray no longer needed that process and grew bored with it.

As previously stated, I was frustrated that the symbol software did not have all the symbols I needed, so I used a borrowed digital camera and took pictures of Billy Ray doing tasks I couldn't find symbols for. Billy Ray's response to the symbols I made with digital pictures was better than to the symbols made with the software.

I started taking pictures of him doing every activity on his schedule. Billy Ray loves having his picture taken for the most part, so he cooperated reasonably well. If he refused to cooperate with a step in the activity, I just took a picture of something that symbolized the activity or used a software symbol for that step.

After being shown what I was doing at home with the picture schedules and activity visuals, the school's autism specialist created a planner for Billy Ray using mostly Boardmaker software symbols. The symbols were printed on about 2- by 2-inch squares that were laminated and had pieces of Velcro on the back. Laminated blank pages with Velcro strips on both sides were spiral-bound. Billy Ray used this, but was not as responsive to computer-generated symbols as he was to my digital pictures.

Given his responsiveness to the picture schedules that I made for him, I started making my own picture symbols and created a planner for him. I no longer do the picture schedules, which he was less responsive to and required more revision to stay current. Since planners have removable symbols they are more flexible. His schedule is set up in the planner very quickly each morning.

See the appendix for instructions on how to make symbols, planners, and picture schedules.

When we began using his planner with picture symbols for activities instead of a schedule, I created activity visuals with pictures and text for every step. I used activity visuals to teach Billy Ray the sequence that we would follow. He loved looking at a picture of himself doing the next step and I would read him the text I had written explaining that step. Before long, we had every step in an activity down to a routine he was comfortable with. A sample of activity visuals appears in the appendix together with instructions on how to make them. More examples can be found on www.parentingyourcomplexchild.com.

After he became familiar with the sequence, the visuals no longer needed to be shown to him. The visuals were put into a notebook and maintained for future reference. They came in handy when teaching the sequences to a new caregiver.

I remembered that Billy Ray used to love carrying one of my old Day-Timer planners that had handles like a briefcase. When he would accompany me to visit clients or for meetings, he would carry it with comic books, coloring books, and markers in it. He called it "my case" (briefcase). We got him a new one as similar to the old one as possible, laminated some colored sheets of paper, adhered Velcro strips to the pages, three-hole-punched them, and put them in the planner case.

ADAPTING TO THE SCHEDULE

Presenting a schedule to your child at the beginning of the day can reduce negative behaviors caused by confusion and the twenty-question routine that drives this parent crazy first thing in the morning. Do whatever works for your child, but go over the schedule with him as early in his day as possible. Sometimes it works best to take Billy Ray's planner into his bedroom if I can get in there before he comes out. Many times this has gotten him out of being "stuck" and refusing all scheduled activities. It takes away the confusion about what his day is going to entail.

As you start this process of encouraging him to participate in his new schedule, expect some reluctance. If you get any participation at all, at least you have something to build on. Be careful to praise your child enthusiastically for the smallest effort. Take the time to note results in your journal as much as you can. It will help you to track progress and to see where you might make changes. After a week of trying the new schedule, look at your notes and ask yourself:

- Does he appear comfortable with the new routine?

- Is there less agitation, refusal, or negative behavior with this routine?

- Are there problem areas that need to be adjusted to make the day flow better or help him to better understand what is expected?

If there are problem areas, adjust your sequence or procedures slightly.

As I introduced new schedules to Billy Ray or made modifications in existing ones, I talked to him as though I expected him to carry on a two-way conversation about his schedule. I asked him questions about his comfort level with the routine and gave him plenty of time to respond. Sometimes he was able to say "yes" or "no" to my questions, other times not. Quiet listening to my questions or comments were considered a positive response if he couldn't get the words out. Agitation or high noise was considered discomfort with what I was saying about his schedule. Of course, the response might have been unrelated to what I was asking, depending upon whether he was in the same place I was or had departed into his own world to escape what I was talking about. It was not always clear. We were talking about his life. I wanted him as involved as possible at every step. On some level I felt he understood that we were trying. As time went on he seemed more eager to participate in these conversations.

As you get a piece or two of the schedule actually working comfortably for your child and you, it might be time to look for help with your complex child a few hours a week so you can have some rest along the way. This enables you to meet some other family-member needs sooner, too. If your child can go to a Saturday respite center for three or four hours, it is a great plan. If not, maybe he can visit grandparents or you can obtain respite care through your local developmental disabilities program. Whether you can do that or not, do not lose hope that you will be able to organize your family life better. It won't happen immediately, but you can do this. Take comfort in that you are changing the things you can—albeit slowly.

There are undoubtedly going to be problem areas that you cannot change. In those cases, adapt as much as you can. Giving Billy Ray his morning pills along with a nutritional supplement is an example. Billy Ray needs the food with the medications but is too active to eat breakfast until he has medication, so you adapt. You will undoubtedly need many of these adaptations in your child's schedule. You'll have areas where you cannot change her, but you can change your method.

Repeat the process you used to create the first part of the schedule to create additional parts of her schedule. When you are ready, start working with her on the new parts of her schedule.

As she gets used to the routine, watch for tasks that she seems independent or nearly independent in doing. For example, could she set the table while you read a story to her sibling or clean her room while you have a bubble bath or spend time with another family member? Could she be trusted to watch a movie while you do some other needed task? As her confidence in knowing what is expected of her builds, you may be able to trust her more. Each complex child is an individual in this regard.

If your child has an escape tendency, for example, you may need to remain in view of her, but you might be able to read a story or play a game with another child across the room.

SHOPPING WITH YOUR CHILD

Shopping can be a major problem with a complex child, especially if he is a "power shopper" and you are on a tight budget. Obviously, shopping is going to be easiest if your child is involved in some other activity and you can go shopping without him. If you work away from home and can do grocery shopping or other major shopping on your way home from work, it might work out best. This is not always possible or feasible. Shopping is a part of life, especially grocery shopping.

If your child will be with you when you're shopping, make all the preparations you can for a successful trip. If possible, visit the store without your child first. Make a list of the aisles you will need to avoid because he will want something you can't buy for some reason (not good for him, too much money, etc.). Make a quick map of the aisles you will go down just like you would make a trip map for a drive in the car. Make a list of planned purchases and discuss it with your child before you leave for the store. Let him make reasonable additions to the list. If possible, set up some reward such as lunch out if you stick to the list and he stays calm. If he is a power shopper, it is going to be cheaper for you to spring for lunch at McDonald's or a family restaurant than to pay for all the stuff he throws in the cart or damages.

An important part of preparation is your choice of store. For example, if your child is really into a specific item and you know that one store will have that item prominently displayed in so many locations you can't possibly avoid it, choose a store that has fewer problem areas. A moderate-size store may have fewer problem areas for your child. It might be more expensive, but if your child is less likely to exhibit difficult behavior and you are less likely to compromise with him to get him out of the store, it might be cost effective. If your child is small enough, you can pick him up to leave; this might be less of an issue than a teenager who throws himself on the floor because he can't understand why you won't buy him everything he wants.

There may be other arrangements you can make for minimizing problems with shopping. For example, Billy Ray loves to buy fresh french bread that comes in paper bags. Our favorite grocery store has a bakery and will have the bread fresh at 5 p.m. each weekday. A bakery clerk wheels a cart all over the store trying to sell loaves, and there are numerous racks around the store at that time of day. If I take Billy Ray into the store, he is going to grab a loaf off each rack we walk by and from the bakery clerk as well. By the time I try to get it away from him he has handled it too much or it has been damaged so we have to buy it. It does not keep well, and he eats very little of it once it is home. We really do not need five loaves of french bread. Instead of changing stores, I talked to the manager about what time of day the racks are out and modified our shopping times accordingly.

As time goes on you will discover which activities you are going to be able to do with your child and which are easier to do without him. Work around those activities as much as you can.

BEDTIME ROUTINES

Review your journal to decide how and when bedtime routines are going to work best for your child and for the rest of the family. Create a routine for that time of day. Sometimes extreme measures have to be taken for children who are unsafe because of escape or self-abuse problems. If you need a monitor in his room or a lock on his door and can do it safely, do what you have to do without feeling guilty. Your child needs to be safe and the rest of the family needs some sleep, too.

Sleep is an area where it has been necessary to make many adaptations in our home. For a while Billy Ray just would not sleep. No amount of medication worked in the long term. We might get a new sleep medication that worked wonderfully for a week or several months, but eventually it stopped working. For several months I put a sleeping bag on the floor in his doorway and slept as much as possible. If he tried to leave his room, he had to walk over me so I knew he was leaving the room. I wrote a visual about being safe at night, which seemed to help some.

We are fortunate in that once Billy Ray is asleep he is trustworthy. He does wake up often in the night, but he will come into our room to get me. Although it is definitely mother-and-child-like, I prefer not to sleep in the bed with him at his present age of twenty-three years. There are nights, however, that I am so exhausted from several nights of interrupted sleep that I crawl in his bed and can sleep with an arm over him even if he is bouncing up and down and noisy. I am aware of his noise and can monitor his actions, but I have learned to sleep with enough awareness to keep him safe. Additionally, if I am in the bed, he will generally stay there too.

PLANNING FOR THE FUTURE

At some point in your child's life, you will want to create a transition plan for when she is ready to leave home or when you are not able to care for her. The purpose of making a transition plan is to ascertain what goals can reasonably be expected in terms of living arrangements and what steps you can take to prepare her for that plan. The timing is difficult. You may not have an accurate picture when a child is too young. If you wait until she is nearly out of school, important skills may be forgotten that could have been goals during school.

We started thinking about this for Billy Ray when he was about two or three years old. We were at a crossroad of sorts, deciding how to use what financial resources we expected to have for his future. He needed more speech therapy than our HMO would cover. This was costing a significant amount of money each month. As a probate paralegal, I knew about special-needs trusts funded by parents' life insurance. We could not afford the premiums for an adequate insurance trust in addition to the monthly cost of speech therapy. We had to decide whether we should pay the premiums for an insurance trust to pay for custodial care for Billy Ray after our deaths or spend the money on speech therapy that might increase his chances at having some degree of semi-independent living as an adult. I asked the pediatrician for a crystal-ball type of opinion.

The pediatrician felt there was a strong chance—given the speed in which Billy Ray seemed to be reaching milestones—that we could expect him to be semi-independent as an adult. Based on that opinion and our own feelings, we continued the speech therapy and took a smaller term life-insurance policy to fund a smaller trust.

Making a concrete plan for a young child is probably too much of a gamble. Neither Raymond nor I nor the pediatrician could have known about the changes in Billy Ray that would occur following his medication reaction. Hope of Billy Ray being even semi-independent has been affected by that event. Having said that, it is never too early to start thinking and making some notes in your journal about planning.

When you are able to get a reasonably clear picture of your child's abilities, you can make a draft transitional plan for your child. It seems like by the time your child is ten or twelve, you could have some idea. If your child is older than that now, start wherever you are. Begin by asking yourself or discussing with your spouse or others questions such as:

- Is it reasonable to expect my child to live independently?
- Would building in supports, such as hiring a semi-independent living provider (SILP) to check on him, offer some training in

basic living skills, and assist with more complicated things, make independent living more likely?

• If a facility is necessary, what type is appropriate?

Check with organizations such as The ARC or your local developmental disabilities program to find out what programs are available in your area. Programs differ in the degree of independence and care provided as well as the necessary abilities on the part of a resident. If you learn of a particular program that you like, be it a semi-independent apartment program or a residential program, ask questions about what your child will need to be able to do independently. Maybe in the apartment program she will have someone to dispense daily medications. In other programs, she might need to be able to take her own medications from bubble packs dispensed by a pharmacy. Generally, look at whether she can be reasonably expected to learn the skills necessary to function in programs you like.

Although available resources change, I would recommend you start looking at them several years before your child is old enough to be transitioned. Exploring helps you create a "dream" for your child, and then you can help her learn skills that will be necessary to achieve those dreams. In the example of taking medication, you would want to work with her at home on learning to dispense her own medications using bubble packs for a long period of time to ensure that she is dependable at performing this important task.

Our plan had to be totally reconsidered at age fifteen because of the changes in Billy Ray. Even then, we couldn't be sure. The pediatrician felt it was most likely he would return to what was normal for him. Although I hoped that would be the case, a year later it did not appear to be happening.

I created a transitional plan for Billy Ray when he was sixteen, anticipating two possibilities for adult living situations. Because we hoped he would return to the high-functioning person he was before his seizures and be able to live in a semi-independent apartment program, I included that as one possibility and made a list of all the skills he would need to do that. I took those skills and broke them down by what the school could teach him, what I would need to teach him at home, and what private training he would need so that he could reach the goals. The other possibility was that he would need to go in a certain group home. Again, we figured out what skills he would need to have for that particular group home—what the school needed to teach him and what we needed to take responsibility for teaching him at home. You can see a part of this plan in appendix figure 11.

This type of transitional plan with a backup plan might be done when a child is much younger, rather than developing a specific plan with all energies being put toward one goal that might turn out to be unrealistic. Figure out the desired goal, then create a backup plan or even two backup plans if there are many unknowns.

Use the transition plan in IEP meetings and service-planning meetings with governmental agencies to show the services your child needs. Review it occasionally to make sure you are on track at home with things you want to teach your child in order to accomplish goals for his adult life. If your child is able to understand, you should discuss the ideas in the transition plan with him. He should have input if he is capable of it.

We will talk specifically about getting professionals to provide services to help your child achieve the goals of the transitional plan in chapter 13, "Getting the Professionals to Listen." In chapter 16, "Mapping the Journey," we will talk more about what you can do over the years to help meet the goals you set.

11

SERVICE DOGS

UNDER THE AMERICANS WITH DISABILITIES ACT (ADA), accommodations are made allowing disabled persons to have service animals. Service dogs are used to assist people in various ways, depending on the needs of the person relying on a service dog. There are:

- Guide dogs for the blind

- Hearing-ear dogs for the deaf

- Mobility dogs that assist people with mobility problems, such as those in wheelchairs

- Seizure dogs that sense when their handlers are about to have a seizure

- Psychiatric dogs

- Service dogs for children with disabilities

As you can see, service dogs are no longer only for blind, deaf, or wheelchair-bound persons. Interest is increasing in providing service dogs to autistic children and those with other disabilities.

In the right situation, service dogs contribute much to the child and his family. A child and his dog communicate in ways that no one else shares. Given the right match, they become soul mates more deeply than words will express. Figure 11.1 demonstrates the old saying that a picture is worth a thousand words. Notice Billy Ray's hand on Sheba's head while the other hand is feeding papers into a shredder. I think the relationship between Billy Ray and his dog really comes through more than I could describe.

Service dogs are not miracle cures for every disabled person. There are many factors to be considered, including, but certainly not limited to, the ability of your child to work with and take care of the dog and the

FIGURE 11.1   Billy Ray and his service dog.

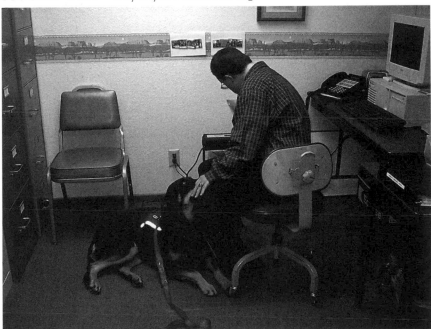

right type of dog for your child. Having a service dog in your home is like having another child in your home. It brings extra stress and adds to the needs of your child and your family. Ideally, your child will learn to manage most of the care for his dog, but there are veterinary appointments and licenses to arrange. Grooming and routine medications for fleas and heartworms are generally something a parent must supervise. There are also the financial considerations.

BILLY RAY'S FIRST DOG

Use of a service dog in Billy Ray's life is another way we have adapted to his needs. We have used a dog with him since he was a toddler, because I am a dog lover. When Billy Ray came to us in 1984, service dogs for developmentally disabled children were not common. When the ADA was enacted in 1990, Billy Ray was already working with his first dog.

We had an old poodle, Pepper, who had been with us for several years. He was a little unsure of this active person we brought into the house, who could crawl faster than most people walk. Pepper had problems with his kneecaps that required us to take hold of his rear legs and pull back so his knees would go back in place. Billy Ray observed us doing that and tried to do it inappropriately. This was obviously painful to Pepper and we feared Billy Ray might get bitten.

The vet said the answer was to get him his own dog so he would be less stress on Pepper. He would need a special kind of dog. It had to have a sturdy bone structure so that it wouldn't be hurt by Billy Ray's active playing, and it needed to be a fairly active dog to tolerate the constant attention. The vet clinic found a five-month-old mixed breed dog named Katie that worked well for him for about twelve years.

Katie was a working dog from the start, but not a designated service dog. It became difficult to get Billy Ray to sleep at night, wake him up in the morning, or even take a bath without his dog nearby. I discussed with Dr. Ron, himself a dog lover, the ways I was using the dog. He said using the dog was a great idea for Billy Ray and encouraged developing his relationship with the dog by having him take as much responsibility for her as he could. He was feeding her when he was only three years old. Billy Ray participated in her puppy obedience classes and training practice right along with me. Some of his first words were dog commands. It was his job to take her for walks (with supervision from one of us) and to feed her. He brushed her and assisted with her baths.

Katie's job was to wake Billy Ray up in the morning. Initially I would say to Katie, "It is time for us to go wake up Billy Ray." She would accompany me for the task, jump up on his bed, and give him puppy kisses, which he loved. Eventually she was beating me to his room every time, so I just said, "Go wake up Billy Ray," which she did while I got out his Boost and morning medication.

After we sold the home we had occupied with my now deceased husband, we looked for an apartment where we could have the dog. We were turned down repeatedly. Then one apartment manager asked if she was a designated service dog. He gave me the regulations surrounding acceptance of tenants' service dogs. Billy Ray's doctor had to prescribe a dog for him just as he would medication. In addition, the veterinarian had to write a letter that said Katie was the right temperament for the task and current on her vaccinations. The team was now legitimate.

Because Katie was growing older and experiencing symptoms common to aging dogs, I began to explore replacing her with a trained service dog. Billy Ray's condition had changed after his medication reaction, and the idea of having a dog assist more in his life seemed worth trying.

TRAINING A SERVICE DOG

At that time, there were not many trainers and service dog organizations available. I did find a man who trained police dogs who said he would train a dog for my son for approximately $10,000. I think the cost of the dog was extra, but I can't recall for sure.

We searched the Humane Society and rescue organizations and let others know we were looking for a dog with the right personality for Billy Ray's needs. Eventually our neighbor, a 4-H leader, found Sheba, believed to be a German shepherd and Doberman mix. Sheba and Billy Ray were a good match. Her mellow temperament had major calming effects for Billy Ray.

Sheba adapted so easily to our obedience training that we searched for someone to train her to be a service dog we could take out in public.

We had seen the calming effect she had on him at home. Billy Ray's agitation was increasing, and taking him out was becoming more of a challenge. Medication did not control his agitation unless he got a high-enough dosage; then he often slept too much. Using Sheba away from home seemed like a good thing to try.

We were able to find one trainer whose experience seemed to be more centered on dogs to assist people in wheelchairs. Her office was in a city about an hour away. We would go there part of the time, but she felt she would need to do part of the training in our home. She would charge travel time at her hourly rate, which was substantial. It was not affordable or practical given the distance.

Using the Internet, I found a trainer who lived in a neighboring state and called her. After I explained that Sheba had been so easy to train that we did not even take her to obedience courses, the woman asked why I hadn't considered training Sheba myself. Her suggestion was to figure out what the dog's job would be and teach her one new environment at a time. She also suggested that we buy her a cape identifying her as a service dog and practice, practice, practice. She made it sound so easy. With Sheba, it actually was easier than with most dogs.

Benjamin, the caregiving assistant who worked with Billy Ray both at home and at school, was experienced with dogs too. As I worked out what activities we would try to involve Sheba in, Benjamin was able to easily put my suggestions into practice. Sheba went to dinner in restaurants with Billy Ray, traveled with us, stayed in motels, etc. We were able to take her anywhere she could be useful to Billy Ray.

Sheba was such a wonderful dog and so useful to Billy Ray, and we worked closely with the veterinarian to treat her deteriorating legs as she grew older. We tried various medications and repeatedly discussed whether surgery was an option. Finally, she was unable to make it up and down the stairs to go out with Billy Ray, so she was no longer useful as a service dog. We kept her as a pet until her suffering seemed cruel, but replaced her as a service dog. That's when we got our current service dog, a Weimaraner named Penny Lane.

IS A SERVICE DOG RIGHT FOR YOUR CHILD?

Obtaining a service dog that is appropriately trained for your child's needs is an involved process. If you were to buy a service dog from a trainer or organization, it would not be unrealistic to expect to pay $10,000 to $15,000 or more. Some trainers will train your own dog if the dog and your child fit the trainer's criteria. Most trainers I talked to said it would be in the neighborhood of $4,000 to $5,000 to train your dog.

Nonprofit organizations and trainers may provide service dogs to disabled persons free or at a reduced rate, but waiting lists can be more than five years. There are differing conditions depending on the program. Some will say that you have to do the fund-raising. This means that you have to solicit funds from charitable organizations in your area that will sometimes give grants for all or part of the cost of the dog and training. Others will provide the dog free of charge but require families to pay their own travel and lodging expenses to the organization's headquarters for training on how to use the dog and for interviews. Some organizations also charge placement fees of approximately $2,500.

The decision about whether a service dog is right for your child should be carefully considered before you try to obtain one. Unless it has a major benefit for your child in terms of calming him, increasing his ability to participate in meaningful activities, reducing your child's risk of escape, or some other significant help, a service dog may not be worth the added effort. Billy Ray's dog has a calming effect on Billy Ray, both at home and in public for the most part. She adds substantial meaning to his life. However, there are also times life would be easier without her.

Think about the following to help you decide whether a dog is appropriate for your child:

- What are the activities you want a dog to assist your child with?
- Can those activities be done with a family pet that doesn't accompany your child into the community in the same way a service dog can?
- What benefit would a service dog have on your child's individual needs? For example, does he need a dog to:
  - Make him feel secure in the community or in school?
  - Keep him calm enough to participate in activities that he would not be able to participate in without a dog?
  - Aid in socialization in the community?
  - Provide some form of medical monitoring or supervision?
- Is your child going to be able to handle a dog without extra supervision in his daily routine?

- Can you afford the extra cost of the dog's care even if you are able to get a service dog through an organization that provides them to disabled children? Arfkids' website suggests a figure of $100 per month for basic food and care. I am not sure that includes routine medications such as flea treatment and heartworm medications. Our costs probably exceed that because of Penny Lane's recurring ear infections. Dogs have medical issues just like children, and theirs usually aren't covered by insurance.

- How will having a dog affect others in the home?

If you have access to the Internet, you can find a lot of information about service dogs on www.arfkids.com and www.deltasociety.org. I have also included some information about service dogs and links on my website, www.parentingyourcomplexchild.com.

MAKING IT WORK

Here are some issues that should be considered carefully when deciding on whether to try a service dog.

The Trainer

There are no uniform standards for service trainers. You should inquire about a trainer's background and success with training dogs to perform the specific tasks your child's dog will be expected to perform. It is with some reluctance that I share our experiences with training service dogs for Billy Ray. Your ability to train your own service dog is directly related to your experience with dogs. I looked at the following factors in considering whether I could train Billy Ray's service dog:

- I had been involved in obedience classes with many dogs over the years and trained other dogs at home.

- The "jobs" we were asking the dog to do primarily involved obedience skills. She would be asked to heel, sit, lie down, and stay as she accompanied Billy Ray in his daily activities. Billy Ray's school participation consisted of modified activities instead of a classroom where he would be taking the dog alone. If we needed her to prevent Billy Ray from running into the street or escaping, I would not feel we had the experience to train her.

- Because of Billy Ray's complexities, he is never alone in the community or at home. He will always have a parent or caregiver with him. Thus, there is support always available in working with the dog.

The Personality of the Dog

The temperamental mismatch between parent and child that we talked about in chapter 8 applies to dog and handler too. Dogs have temperamental characteristics too. If they are to become soul mates of sorts, child and dog must be comfortable with each other. Some of your child's behavior might frighten the most mellow, loving dogs, especially if she is noisy or makes sudden movements. Other dogs will tolerate the behavior well.

We often laugh about how Billy Ray's present service dog, Penny Lane, is a good match for him because she has autistic-like tendencies too. She gets used to routine. She has a built-in planner. She knows when it is time to eat or do some activities. She tries to get her own leash out of the drawer when she knows it is time to go somewhere. Billy Ray and Penny Lane keep each other on schedule well.

Finally, the dog must be trustworthy. You have to look at the risk the dog and child present to each other. When Billy Ray is frustrated, he may express that by punching. The two most likely victims are his Mom and his dog because he feels safest with us. The punches are not hard enough to hurt either of us. If his dog were small, this would be a greater concern. Nevertheless, a dog bite has always been something I have feared. Fortunately, all three of Billy Ray's dogs have been tolerant. However, Sheba became afraid of him toward the end of her life—probably because of her deteriorating health—and it affected their relationship. She was always willing to go places with him, but avoided him at home on occasion.

Penny Lane seems totally tolerant and unafraid. She and Billy Ray are total soul mates. The vet once laughed that she has got him figured out. He might punch her on rare occasions, but he is good for a treat anytime. Penny Lane actually "trained" Billy Ray to open the door to the cabinet where her food and treats are kept. One day I came out of the bathroom and discovered him getting her an extra treat. Now we have to really watch her weight because she knows how to work her owner so well.

I think that Penny Lane just accepts things from Billy Ray she would not accept from the rest of us. Early on in her time with him, they were both at the dining room table as I was clearing it. She was in a sit position next to him. He wiped his mouth and hands with his napkin, then proceeded to wipe her mouth with his napkin. She sat there calmly allowing it. I actually tried to wipe her mouth one time when she was dripping water on my clean floor. She refused to allow me to do it. She seems to understand Billy Ray and is not afraid of him.

The Handler

The degree of competency required of your child as the handler depends on how independent your child is. If your child is going to school on his own or is performing some other independent activities with the dog, he is probably prepared to be in control of his dog. If your child requires constant supervision, you, your spouse, other family members, or the caregiver will have to assist with handling the dog.

The Community's Reaction

The ADA grants equal access to what might be a hostile community for your child. When you add a service dog, that hostility can increase. Property owners are legally required to allow a disabled person to have a service dog on the property. But some will make it known that they resent being required to allow a dog for a disabled person in a "no pets allowed" building. Some landlords simply will find other reasons not to rent to your family.

Public reaction to service dogs is mixed, just as acceptance of your child's right to equal access is mixed. Acceptance of your child walking with her service dog on the street or a park is generally good. If your child and her dog walk into a restaurant or grocery store, people may stare and remarks may be made. Laws mandating acceptance of service dogs fail to control fear in some people. If certain facilities and businesses do not present an accepting environment for your child and her service dog, try to use the principles in chapter 14, "Creating a Community for Your Child," to find welcoming environments.

BEFORE YOU TAKE THE PLUNGE

It is well worth the time to investigate whether a service dog is right for your child before you put the effort into securing one. If you have a dog or have access to friends or family members who have a dog you can use, you might try some experimentation with the dog and your child. If you know someone going on vacation, you could offer to dogsit and then see how things work out between your child and the dog. You can explain to your child that he is babysitting the dog for Grandma or for some friend. That way, he is more likely to understand he has to give the dog back than if you bring a dog home from the Humane Society or a rescue organization.

A word of caution: Bringing a hyperactive dog into the house may actually agitate your child. The dog's personality is an important part of the experiment too. A dog your child knows well is best. A dog that is familiar with your house and family is even better.

Try having your child pet the dog when he is agitated. Does it calm him? If he is stuck or in some power struggle, ignore the behavior he is stuck in and suggest he do something with the dog, even if it is just giving the dog a treat. Experiment with having the dog participate in waking the child up and putting him to bed or during other stressful times. Try involving the dog in any activity that you have noted as problematic in your journal. Does having the dog sleep with your child positively or negatively affect his sleeping? Observe whether having the dog present has a calming effect or is more stressful to your child. If he has an appointment that he normally resists, suggest taking the dog with you at least in the car. Note his reaction to having the dog near.

A good test is if your child is stressed about going to the doctor's office or the lab for blood work. Ask the doctor in advance for an opinion about the appropriateness of a service dog for your child. Tell the doctor you would like to experiment with using one. Technically, because the dog is not yet a service dog, you cannot take him into such settings. However, the doctor can arrange permission for such trials.

If a dog is not available and you are determined to try, call your local veterinarian or rescue organization. Explain to them that you are considering a service dog for your child. Avoid promising to adopt the dog, but leave that option open. You might also contact your local Humane Society. I suspect they would want more assurance that you will keep the dog, but it is worth trying.

If you decide to "borrow" a dog to experiment with, be sure to investigate the dog thoroughly unless it is a dog you are quite familiar with. Visit the dog without your child first. Observe the dog's personality traits, including fearfulness. Dogs that are frightened can become aggressive. Spend enough time with the dog to determine if it is excited by the attention generated by your visit (which would be natural) or if it is consistently excitable or hyperactive. Depending on your child's personality, an excitable or hyperactive dog might overstimulate him. Visit again with the child before bringing the dog home even for a visit.

If you decide a service dog is worth the effort, speak to your child's doctor about whether an order for a service dog is prudent. As of this writing, all that is required to designate a service dog is an order by the doctor and a letter by a veterinarian that the dog is healthy, current on its vaccinations, and of the right temperament. There is current discussion about certification being required for service animals because of the abuse that has occurred. Some people have even used minihorses, pigs, cats, etc., as service animals, which has caused the use of service animals to come under some scrutiny. It is expected that at some point laws will be modified to include only certified service animals.

ADAPTING TO THE SERVICE DOG

We have adapted the use of Billy Ray's service dog just as we adapted visuals or other approaches to work for him. The doctor's prescription says that Billy Ray should be allowed to take his dog everywhere because she reduces his agitation. That is accurate overall. However, there are times that the dog can make a situation worse. Billy Ray's need for the dog changes, depending on factors such as his health. As he has had to replace dogs, the different dogs have been more useful in different ways.

His first dog was a pet but helped him sleep. We took her with him when we traveled because she helped him go to sleep in motels and stay calm in the car. The second dog, Sheba, was very mellow and able to be used in public settings with ease. We are still in the process of training Billy Ray's present dog, Penny Lane, to be more useful as a service dog. However, it is clear that she will not be as useful in certain settings as Sheba. On the other hand, Billy Ray and Penny Lane are even more soul mates than Sheba and Billy Ray were. Their temperaments match very well.

More important are the natural skills that Penny Lane has demonstrated that neither of Billy Ray's previous dogs demonstrated. Occasionally Billy Ray has experienced shallow breathing, which has concerned us greatly. When we notice this, we can wake him and he will resume breathing normally. On several occasions since getting Penny Lane, she has come to get me. Her credibility at such times is good. If she brings me to Billy Ray's room, he needs help. It is freeing to know that she is watching him. Penny Lane enables me to have chats with my husband and complete necessary tasks instead of monitoring Billy Ray as closely. He is sleeping longer hours at night with her, and I can rest knowing she will come and get me if needed.

At the time we got Penny Lane, Billy Ray was experiencing a series of health issues. We have not trained Penny Lane fully to work with Billy Ray in public because of his inability to be out in public. Now that he is stronger physically, we are working with her.

Do what works for your child and the family. If having a service dog as your child's constant companion seems appropriate, adapt its use to meet your child's needs. If your child does not seem responsive to the presence of a dog, it may not be something you want to try.

CHAPTER

12

DOCUMENT EVERYTHING

THE IDEA BEHIND my documentation and advocacy methods is to communicate what your child experiences to the professionals and others involved with her in the most realistic way possible. It takes time to accomplish and sounds overwhelming. But dealing with side effects from medications that were inappropriate to begin with or educational services that frustrate your child takes time and can be overwhelming too. Communicating your child's needs accurately so that she gets the right services and medications to begin with saves frustration and may actually save time.

Let me summarize the purposes of putting your limited energy into documenting everything:

- Documentation helps you to see a pattern of what works and what might trigger undesirable results.

- You are able to give the doctor more information in a very short amount of time than you could possibly relate verbally, especially if your child is present and creating a problem.

- The doctor's decisions regarding medication or other recommendations for treatment will be informed decisions. Without a clear understanding of your child, recommendations for treatment are a gamble at best.

- Documentation sometimes also demonstrates that side effects from medications may be occurring that might not have been obvious otherwise. For example, you can demonstrate medical issues that started shortly after starting a certain medication.

- Having this complete history of what has been done becomes important in unexpected ways.

- Documentation demonstrates what your child is able to do and in what areas she needs services.

- It gains you respect for knowing your child and helps you to be heard when trying to be her advocate. Frankly speaking, most professionals are impressed. That usually makes a big difference in the "dumb-parent treatment."

- Documentation saves time and frustration.

- It becomes a part of estate planning for your child so that you are able to communicate her needs even when you aren't available to take care of her.

You can make documentation as simple as possible or it can be more involved. That decision should be based on what you are trying to communicate about your child and the amount of time you can spend on documentation. If your child functions consistently, you may be able to write in the journal or progress note form every few days and yearly, near her birthday, update your abbreviated chronology of events so you have a brief history. If you are trying to demonstrate specific symptoms or behaviors to the doctor, you may need to make a daily note in the journal (do not count on your memory), then prepare brief summaries for the doctor. I make a series of documents that help me to gather data.

JOURNAL OR PROGRESS NOTES

I started this by just adding it to my own journal when we adopted Billy Ray. If your child has limited changes and you already keep a journal, that works fine. If you do not keep a journal, you could get a spiral notebook and keep notes of doctor's visits and significant events. However, if your child has regular visits to the doctor, is on medications, has sleep issues, medical problems, or problem behaviors at home or at school, you probably need a journal especially for him.

I started a spiral notebook after the psychiatrist began asking what a day in Billy Ray's life was like. I wrote in it after I came out of his room from tucking him in at night. When we were going to the doctor, I took the notebook with me to refer to. Many times I was able to answer questions that I would not have been able to if I didn't have his journal. Referring to the journal for questions while you are with the doctor can be time consuming and disruptive to the flow of the visit if you have several pages over which to search for information.

After Billy Ray's sleep issues worsened so that he would not stay in bed unless I was in his room, I put my old computer in his room. It served the dual purpose of being an educational tool for him and a way for me to do some of the work involved in his care while I needed to be in his room. I am able to make notes of the day or prepare his documentation for appointments during time that would otherwise be spent watching Disney movies with him for the umpteenth time.

If you use a computer for the journal, print it out weekly or monthly and put it in a notebook. If you have in-home caregivers who don't use the computer, have them keep progress notes on notebook paper or a form you create and copy. You can add your own notes in the same notebook.

I also use the journal notebook as a sort of file for records. Our HMO gives summaries of each office visit and sends us lab results. I put them next to the journal page for the same date. At the end of the year when I update his abbreviated history, that notebook can be put away and a new one started. Alternatively, the contents can be removed from the notebook and put in a file folder for the past year and the notebook reused for the next year.

Examples of things to note in the journal are:

- Medical issues (even routine colds). If they occur regularly, it may indicate a problem of some other nature. This might include bowel issues if your child is prone to those.

- Negative behaviors, including those the doctor might be tracking or you are trying to demonstrate as a pattern that needs to be addressed. If it is something you are tracking, you might underline or highlight it with a specific color so you can easily glean it later.

- School issues. Often there is a take-home communication book between school and home. If that is the case, you may not need to detail problems in your child's journal, but make a note to remind yourself to look under the date in the school's communication book. If you have a conversation with the teacher about some issue other than what is in the school's book, make note of it in your home journal.

In chapter 8, I gave you figure 8.1 as an example of journal entries in a more routine time. Figure 12.1 is an example from Billy Ray's journal during a rough period. The notes are more detailed because it was clear something was going on and I wanted to track it. On a routine day, I might write nothing more than that he participated with his schedule well and how long he slept.

MEDICATION SCHEDULE

I make a list of Billy Ray's medication on the computer because it is easier to revise (we have so many changes). I put a printout in the journal by the date of the change. I also post a printout on the inside of the cupboard where I keep Billy Ray's medication. This list serves many purposes:

- I have a history of Billy Ray's medications, which is helpful when that information is requested.

- Family and caregivers are accurate and consistent with administering medications.

- Taking a copy with me to doctor's appointments or other situations where I need to report current medications is a lot easier than trying to remember and go over the medications verbally.

FIGURE 12.1   A sample from Billy Ray's journal.

\multicolumn{2}{JOURNAL FOR}	
\multicolumn{2}{7/14/99 through _____}	
DATE	COMMENTS
7/14/99	Agitated in a.m. and manic episodes of hitting, throwing things at me. Tried to pull my chair over. Gave (agitation medication) at 8 a.m. Seemed tired but didn't go to sleep when he lay down at 11 a.m.
	Took staff and BR with me for banking and shopping for bigger clothes for him and groceries. Planned that he would put pop cans in machine, which he enjoys doing. Given (agitation medication) at 12 for signs of escalating agitation. Loading pop cans into van at 12:30 and left for outing. Did well at the restaurant for lunch. Staff commented that getting out really calms him.
	To Wal-Mart. Seemed agitated with staff in parking lot, negative talking, resistance to attempts on staff's part to walk with him, kicking, hitting, pushing staff. Cued to calm down or we wouldn't be able to look for sweat pants and new shoes. Did calm down somewhat and focused on choosing sweats. Tried on several pair of shoes. I would have him walk away and come back to see if the shoes slip on his narrow ankles. He came back appropriately 3 times. The fourth time he took off running to the other end of aisle where some shoes were on the floor and started throwing them at a shopper (an old man), then ran ahead and started kicking and hitting him. The only thing that saved us was this old man was there with another disabled person (his son?) and was fairly understanding. This incident was 2-1/2–3 hours after agitation medication, which normally calms him and lasts 5–6 hours. Fairly agitated the rest of the day. Went to sleep normally but woke up at 11 p.m. for about an hour and then slept until 6 a.m.
7/15/99	Woke up wild, throwing map (rug) at me, taking off his dirty clothes and throwing them at me, hitting, kicking, punching me. Given agitation medication with his regular meds. Calmed down by the time staff arrived at 8:45. Sleeping at 9:20 a.m. Escalating a lot by 4:30—repeated agitation meds. Refused to cooperate with structured teaching or any tasks today. Very restless and agitated. Difficult to get to settle down to sleep but slept all night.
7/16/99	Woke up at 6:30 a.m. manic most of the morning but interested in picking up sticks outside. Tried a task list instead of the cards; seemed more interested in that method. Short nap early afternoon. Took him to get mail, a milkshake treat for outside tasks, and to dinner at his favorite restaurant. We met the owner of the restaurant coming out as we were going in; he said, "Hi guy," to which BR reached up and pushed him hard, literally pinning him against the wall. Agitation meds at 7 a.m., 11 a.m., 3:15 p.m., and 8 p.m. for agitation.
	Note: we have had two major aggressive incidents in 3 days. Going out has always de-escalated him before. Something is changing.

ROUTINE TRACKING FORM

This is an informal chart to note normal and as-needed medications given, sleep (including extra naps during the day), bowel movements, or appetite (if these need to be tracked). You can include this information in your journal instead of having a separate page, but I find having this page makes it easier to glean the information later. I have created a blank spreadsheet for this purpose, and I put it in the front of the journal notebook until the end of the month it is tracking.

A sample of the routine tracking form is in appendix figure 5. You could put it in front of the journal notes in your notebook as I do. An alternative would be to use the combination form (see appendix figure 6), which contains the routine tracking form on the top and room for journal entries on the bottom half. If your normal journal notes are longer, you may find this alternative easier because there would be one page for each day.

SUMMARY

The summary is a brief table or spreadsheet summarizing your child's functioning for the period between appointments with the doctor(s). Focus your summary on whatever the main issues are that you deal with. For example, Billy Ray's summary points are generally sleep and behavior. My summary includes medication changes and physical symptoms as well because of the impact they have on his sleep and behavior. I recommend writing these summaries at least quarterly, whether you see the doctor that often or not, because it helps catch patterns and it is less work when you finally sit down to do it.

The idea behind this document is to get needed information to the doctor or other professional in a format he or she can absorb quickly. It is a summary and therefore it is not heavy with details that take a long time to read or relate verbally. However, it has enough information to answer questions about how he is sleeping (such as whether sleep medications are needed or present ones are working) and how his behavior is (for example, is a medication adjustment needed at this time). If your child is having physical symptoms, they can be demonstrated quickly with the summary. If symptoms coincide with medications, particularly new ones, the summary might alert the doctor to review the medication.

Most doctors and other professionals appreciate the time you have taken to create this summary, and they recognize that it makes things easier for them. I have had several doctors say to me, "I wish all parents made it this simple." One even told me that it made appointments go so much smoother, that if all parents did it this way he might get home to his own family in time for dinner more often. See appendix figure 7 for a partial sample summary. You can get blank forms on my website, www .parentingyourcomplexchild.com, or create your own.

You may wonder why just keeping the brief summary for the doctor might not be enough instead of the journal. The journal keeps the details. There are times you need that much detail.

What you include in the summary depends on your child. You may need to include things at one point that you do not need to every time. For example, if the doctor wants to monitor weight or blood pressure, you may track that during some periods but not others. Include columns for areas that are a concern for your child.

If you are monitoring behavior, it is good to include an "Events/ Stressors" column because behaviors can be caused by numerous things. The behavior might also be caused by a medical problem or related to medication. Include the information in that column when new medication is started.

I prefer to do my summary documents in a spreadsheet or chart with a landscape format. You can also create a handwritten summary by drawing a chart, using four- or five-column ledger paper from an office supply store, or by making one on your computer.

To prepare the documentation, gather your child's journal and the routine tracking forms. If you have not already highlighted and used the little flags suggested in chapter 8, do it now. Mark all the events of aggression in one color, and make a note in the margin about the severity if it isn't noted in the journal itself. Preparing the summary is easier if you have done the highlighting as you go along or at least once a week. If you try to do it at the last minute (say, the night before an appointment), it seems more overwhelming. Reviewing your journal weekly and highlighting things helps you to be more aware of patterns and it makes completing this document easier. Transfer the information to the summary form.

I also prepare a "caveat" that I routinely attach to the summaries. The doctor may not review it each time, but it is available if needed. The caveat is a definition of terms as I use them. It is my experience that even medical professionals use terms differently on occasion. I am aware that my medical terminology is not entirely accurate. Complex children experience symptoms somewhat differently too. This clarification helps make that point relative to an individual child. The important thing is that the doctor knows what you mean. Once you do this, it can be copied and attached each time without redoing it. You can also print it on the back of the first sheet of your summary or photocopy it on the back side of the sheet.

Here is a partial example from my documentation:

TERMS USED IN THIS DOCUMENT

- *Mild Aggression:* Slight punch, almost playfully.

- *Moderate Aggression* ("Mod"): Scratch, pinch, punch that can be felt, but not hard enough to hurt someone; generally to the arm or hand of other person; pushing, but not so hard as to hurt someone.

- *Severe Aggression:* Hard pushes—sometimes hard enough for someone to fall. Punches hard enough to be felt—more often to head or stomach, kicking, scratching. Stabbing with a fork—no matter how much pressure, because we consider it dangerous. Throwing objects at someone.

- *Agitation:* Irritated, nervous, and resistant—even to normal things that he needs to do, such as going to an appointment, even toileting. He can become highly agitated even about something he really wants to do. This sometimes runs into manic; other times is just noisy and irritated. He can "get stuck" in this phase over something that confuses him.

- *Restlessness:* An inability to stay focused on anything for even short amounts of time, walking away from whatever he is doing, pacing the floor as though he is just looking for something to throw or get into.

- *Hyperactivity:* A basic inability to sit still or remain focused on anything. It includes bouncing up and down in place or running and throwing behaviors. Note that some of these behaviors are also a part of mania as we experience it. The main difference is the degree of excitement involved. Hyperactivity can quickly escalate into mania for Billy Ray.

- *Mania*: Similar to the mania in adults (sense of being invincible, no impulse control), but it also includes the following:
  - Hitting, kicking, pushing.
  - General silliness that is out of control.
  - Running from us, both outside or taking off across the room to grab something.
  - Throwing things down the stairwell or just aimlessly across the room. This can be anything he sees sitting on the kitchen counter, clothes from his hamper, his shoes, garbage, etc., particularly something that is out of its normal place. We had to take his wastebasket out of his room because it seemed he couldn't stand even small amounts of trash in it. Now he is beginning to do the same with kitchen garbage.

Before a doctor's appointment, I prepare a packet for the doctor, which includes the summary on top and current list of medications. I like to take an extra copy of the summary report with me so I can refer to it and answer anything the doctor inquires about. I also take the journal pages for the period covered when we see the doctor, in case he wants more details. Because they are color coded, I can quickly find the incidents to answer any questions the doctor has.

ABBREVIATED HISTORY OF DEVELOPMENT, BEHAVIOR, AND TREATMENT

I started making this document when we were getting "second opinions." It is a way of quickly conveying medical history to a busy professional. It also saves you from having to admit you can't remember, when a doctor asks if you have tried a certain treatment and what the results were. The first one I created took a lot of time because I had several years to document. But it should take little time if you use the summaries and medication schedules for the year and complete the history near your child's birthday every year.

I have found this document especially helps me when I am asked questions by doctors about past treatment trials. Appendix figure 8 provides a partial sample of this history. Blank forms to help you start one of your own history can be printed from my website or you can easily create your own. I have removed most of the medication names because I do not want to tempt anyone to try medications that we have tried. Not all medications work for every child. Some work for one child but cause major side effects for other children.

TASK LIST

This is primarily of interest to educational and social-work professionals; however, occasionally it will be requested by doctors as well. Having tasks that your child is able to do written down is much easier than trying to verbalize during meetings. It also demonstrates the degree of independence your child is capable of. Appendix figure 9 is a partial sample.

COMPARISONS

When I am trying to demonstrate some change in Billy Ray's functioning, whether it is from growth or problem areas, I will occasionally do a comparison. This document compares his functioning at one point to his functioning at another point. This is not a document that you need to create unless your child is changing, but it can be useful when necessary. Appendix figure 10 provides a sample.

As you are gathering documentation, some sort of method of organizing helps. I have the current documents filed in notebooks. At the end of the year (it could be your child's birthday or the end of a calendar year—whenever you plan to update the history), I remove the contents after I transfer information to the history. I put the contents of the notebook in a file marked with the year and file it in my file cabinet. As an alternative, you could just place the notebook marked with the year on a bookcase and start a new notebook for the next year.

GETTING THE
PROFESSIONALS TO LISTEN

WE DISCUSSED the "dumb-parent treatment" in chapter 6. As stated, you should not have to prove your child's capabilities to the professionals involved. In fairness to the professionals, however, you do have to consider the following:

- If your child refuses to cooperate or "perform" as well at school as she does at home, the professionals have reason to doubt the abilities you claim she has.

- It is a natural for parents to see their children in the best light; not all reports made by parents are realistic assessments of a child's capabilities.

- People, not robots, administer the laws and regulations relative to appropriate services and/or education for special-needs children. They have their own struggles providing services to your child and in their personal lives.

My friend Heidi Schack, director of special education at Silver Falls School District in Silverton, Oregon, uses the following hypothetical situation to illustrate the difficulty educators may have in understanding that a child is capable of more than he demonstrates in school:

Suppose a parent insists that her child can swim, but every time the school tries to take him swimming he starts to drown. It would be hard to accept the parent's claim. Sometimes you just have to help the professionals to see your child more clearly.

I didn't start the visual and other communication systems shared herein to prove anything to the school professionals. I started them to communicate with my own son. However, it turned out that the visuals and the documentation demonstrated my son's capabilities in ways that I could never have had communicated verbally. They also helped the professionals stop long enough to consider what I was saying.

ESTABLISHING A RELATIONSHIP

You do not need to become best friends with team members, but having a friendly relationship makes it easier to accomplish goals for your child. For example, some parents go overboard with goodies and false appreciation to teachers, etc. Try not to overdo this kind of thing because it appears insecure and insincere. Instead, attempt to find some common ground with the individual. Maybe the teacher is particularly good at getting your child to do some particular thing and you can praise him or her for that. You might occasionally have your child make his teacher something at home that demonstrates ability. That is different than the proverbial apple for the teacher.

Billy Ray and I make cinnamon rolls using the bread dough I learned to make as a young child with my grandmother. When we give them to a teacher or some other professional, I include a note stating the parts of the task he participated in, such as kneading the dough or spreading the butter on it. Sometimes I snap a digital picture of him kneading the dough. Not only does this verify his skill, but teachers, etc. may consider it a special keepsake.

Another time Billy Ray and I were learning to can green beans that Larry grew in the garden, and we gave quarts to his psychiatrist and his teacher.

As a general rule this serves several purposes: it makes the professional feel special, it demonstrates skills that may not be obvious to the professional, and often it is a turning point in getting them to look at your child in a more positive light.

Establishing a nonthreatening relationship with professionals whom you have been in a power struggle with is difficult. If you can do so, it is a fresh start. I know it does not seem fair that you have to be the one to put out the olive branch or peace offering. Keep thinking only about becoming a team with the professionals for the benefit of your child. Do your best to forget about the unfairness. Let it go for the sake of your child.

CREATING A LIST OF GOALS

Once you have had an opportunity to look at your child's strengths and weaknesses by experimenting as we discussed in chapter 8, and you have begun working to improve your relationship with team members, review your child's IEP. Consider whether she is getting the appropriate education and other services. If possible, make a photocopy of the IEP so that you can mark up one copy with changes that you think are needed in terms of life skills and academic skills.

Make a list of any goals you would like added to the plan and your concerns about any existing goals. Resist the temptation to shoot for the moon with too many far-advanced goals. You are more likely to get cooperation if you keep the changes as reasonable as possible, at least while you are trying to rebuild your relationship with the team. Later on, you can ask for other meetings as needed.

After you have made the goals list, think about information you need to support the changes and goals you would like in the plan. If you have pictures of your child doing tasks that demonstrate similar or beginning skills needed to accomplish the goals you will request, use them as support. These illustrate that she has some basic capability or experience to grow from. If there are notes in your journal that you can highlight, they may be helpful too.

If you have made the transitional plan we discussed in chapter 10, it can be used to develop the IEP and to create a list of goals that the school needs to help your child accomplish.

In the transitional plan I did for Billy Ray, I was not able to be definite about his future planning because we had hoped he would recover from the effects of his medication reaction. Thus, I had two possibilities: that he would live in a semi-independent apartment program or, if he was not able to do that, in a certain group home. I made a list of the skills I knew he would need for semi-independent apartment programs from my experience with clients in that type of program. I was less sure about the group home I saw as an alternate plan, so I called them to discuss what level of independence he would need in that setting. A partial sample of the goals list and the transitional plan is shown in appendix figure 11.

To give you an idea of how this planning for the future works, let's take one example:

If Billy Ray were to live in his own apartment and a skills trainer checked on him regularly, he would have a high degree of independence. One of the most important things he would need to do is learn to take his medication independently. At the time I was developing the plan, Billy Ray was very responsible about taking his medications and we did not ever have to worry about him getting into the supply and taking medications inappropriately.

If Billy Ray was going to handle this task, two skills would have to be taught. First, the school would need to teach him to tell time so that he would know when to take his medications. Plus, he had not been taught complete number recognition in school. This was a goal I had fought for before, but I failed to convince the team he was capable of achieving it. I had given him some training at home with flash cards, but this skill would need to be enhanced for him to accurately tell time. Secondly, we would need to start ordering his medications in bubble packs. He would need to be taught to remove his pills from the bubble packs and take them independently.

We could have a backup plan if he could not learn to tell time well enough to know when to take his pills. We could work out some form of alarm system to go off when it was time to take his pills. He would need to have training, probably at home, to use that alarm system.

To create the goals for school and home, I went over the list of everything he would need to do in a semi-independent apartment or the group home, and I made a list of skill goals to take to the planning meeting. See appendix figure 11.

PRESENTING YOUR PLAN

Present your plan or list of skill goals to the IEP team at a meeting you have specially requested for that purpose or at a routine meeting. Tell the teacher or team leader ahead of time that you plan to introduce it at the meeting, so enough time is set aside to discuss it adequately—and so you don't surprise the other team members.

Start by sending a letter to the teacher or other appropriate professional on the IEP team by regular mail. (You don't want to run the risk of losing the letter in your child's backpack.) Keep a copy for your file and note the date mailed. Keep it simple, such as, "I have been reviewing Johnny's IEP. I would like to meet to review Johnny's goals and his progress." If you have difficulty with meetings being scheduled at times when it is hard for you to attend, you might add a list of times you would be available.

Once the meeting is scheduled, do your best to prepare. When I started trying to turn the planning around for Billy Ray, I used my word processor's agenda template. I filled in who was going to attend and what I wanted to discuss. It took less than five minutes.

Generally, my personal agenda is not on that template. It is a list entitled "Things I Want to Discuss in the (date) IEP Meeting." I attach evidence that I want to present in support of modifying the goals. If I do not have specific documentation as evidence, I do a brief outline of reasons of why I think certain goals should be modified. I make a copy for everyone attending. You could make copies at the school before the meeting if the cost or availability of a photocopier is a problem, but walking in with your handouts already prepared gives a good impression and causes less distraction in the beginning of the meeting.

Spend some time preparing yourself. Do what you need to do to build your confidence. Although you shouldn't need to be dressed up for an IEP meeting, if it makes you feel more confident, find a way to spend extra time on your appearance.

After formalities at the beginning of the meeting, you will likely be able to give the reasons for requesting the meeting. Take a deep breath and/or say a quick silent prayer, whatever it takes to calm you as much as possible. State that you have been looking at the IEP and feel the team needs to take another look. Pass out the packets you have prepared.

Start talking about the first goal or change you are requesting, give your reasons, and explain any documentation you have provided to support a change. If things start to get awkward, take another breath and go over your position in some other way if possible. Remind yourself that if a power struggle starts, nothing will change for your child. When it is over, whether you have gotten everything you hoped for or just had one goal agreed to, thank everyone for coming and for listening.

When a plan for your child's future is presented in a way that shows you know your child well and have thought it through, several positive things usually occur:

- The "dumb-parent treatment" tends to change rather quickly, and you build respect.

- Very often, the team begins to see your child in a new light too.

- Professionals enjoy looking at your child's future and feeling the things they do now will make a difference in his success. That is what they hope to do by their work, but presenting your plan in this way helps make it more of a reality to them.

The first time I used this procedure, I remember the principal saying, "I'm impressed" about my preparation. It was a turning point of sorts. The professionals were able to see that I understood my child and that my requests were reasonable. It was worth the effort to get Billy Ray's education actually moving along instead of remaining stuck in a power struggle.

STAYING ON TOP OF THINGS

Once you have established a relationship with the professionals on the team and agreed upon goals that you feel are appropriate for your child, it is important to stay on top of things to ensure progress is occurring and follow-through is happening. Call the teacher, case manager, or other professional on the team to check on how your child is progressing on the goals or whether the team is getting things done that were agreed on.

The school take-home journal is a great avenue for asking about your child's progress if you can't tell by the progress reports the teacher writes. Often schools provide a steno pad and create this communication on their own. If they do not suggest it, purchase a steno pad or some type of spiral bound book and hand it to the teacher. Ask her to occasionally write notes about your child's progress and about any events that you need to know about. Tell her you will send communications from home in this book too.

If the teacher reports difficulty with your child or the goals for her, make it a point to discuss the problem or offer to come in for a meeting. Maybe the two of you can brainstorm to work out the problem. If that does not work, request another meeting to determine whether appropriate steps to achieve the goals are being taken or whether the goal is unrealistic.

Acknowledging your mistakes—if the goal you requested is inappropriate—is freeing to the teacher or case manager because then he or she feels more comfortable acknowledging mistakes as well. Open communication on behalf of the child achieves success better than protecting yourself does. If you are frustrated, admit you are frustrated with your child's lack of progress. Unless you are sure people are dropping the ball, assure them that you realize they are doing what was agreed upon, but it just does not seem to be working for your child. Share a moment of frustration, then start over to plan new goals for your child. The situation does not need to become a blame game.

MEDICAL PROFESSIONALS

When you are trying to get a medical professional to listen to you, you should handle your interaction somewhat differently than with those directly on your child's IEP team. However, some of the same principles apply. You will still want to develop a good working relationship with the doctor or other medical professional, and you need to be prepared. The methods for preparing are different:

- If you are working with the doctor on treating behaviors or specific medical problems, complete the summary packet we talked about in chapter 12. This will help the doctor to see progress and problems between appointments.

- If you are working with a new doctor, attach an abbreviated chronological history or, better yet, mail it to him or her before the first appointment.

Most doctors appreciate the brief summaries that answer their questions quickly. They may not need all this information but will appreciate having it available for future reference if nothing else. As with educational and case-management professionals, this approach tends to show the doctor how well you know your child.

With medical professionals, the follow-up is based on instructions the doctor gives you, such as return appointments or things that you should do or monitor.

CONVINCING EMERGENCY ROOM DOCTORS YOUR CHILD IS REALLY SICK

Some complex children are not able to communicate verbally when they are in pain or tell you where it hurts. Sometimes the only way they have to communicate it is with various types of behavior or agitation. Other times they may say "ouch" but not be able to explain.

Doctors who see your child regularly know more about your child's credibility relative to pain. Emergency room doctors have seldom seen your child before. Your child may be sincerely in pain or simply be a complainer. You may be a parent who has good insight into your child or one who exaggerates. The doctor may have difficulty understanding the situation.

There are all kinds of stories floating around about how doctors don't care about disabled children, especially those on government health-care plans that the hospital will lose money on. I am not going to deny those situations exist in certain instances.

There are clearly two sides to the story. The important issue to deal with here is getting the doctor to see that your child is sick. In that regard, I want to share a recent experience we had in the emergency room.

Billy Ray had been ill for a couple of weeks. He had been closely monitored by our community clinic, which had been very thorough. There were numerous infections taking place at one time. Because of the antibiotics he was taking, lab results—which might have shown what was going on internally—were not giving an accurate picture. The emergency room doctor repeatedly stated that there was no medical reason for his agitation or complaints of pain. He was planning to send him home on psychiatric medications for the agitation.

I could feel the anger welling up inside of me. Having had a similar experience before, where a different emergency room called the security guard at the first sign of anger, I knew I had to stay cool. I also knew that Billy Ray was more ill than I had ever experienced. I sensed that how I handled the next few minutes was a matter of life or death for my son.

Billy Ray was asleep because of intravenous pain medication the doctor had given him. I asked the nurse to watch him and went outside for a break. Team-building advocacy was absolutely vital at that moment, even though what I wanted to do was blow up.

After regrouping, I walked back into the emergency room and tried to establish some common ground with the doctor. I recognized that he had an emergency room full of patients and that Billy Ray was hard to diagnose because he couldn't communicate what was going on with him. I explained to the doctor that there are two kinds of agitation Billy Ray exhibits: one when he has mental confusion and another when he is in pain. Finally, I told the doctor that a surgeon who had lanced a cyst on Billy Ray's leg had stated that Billy Ray must have a high tolerance for pain in order to endure the pain of that cyst.

Following our conversation, the doctor ordered a CAT scan of Billy Ray's abdomen, which showed an enlarged pancreas and appendicitis that was leaking bacteria into his abdomen. He also had some major gastritis and the beginnings of an ulcer. A surgeon was called in and Billy Ray was taken to emergency surgery late that Saturday night.

The importance of team-building advocacy is demonstrated in this situation. Whether the doctor is trying to rush your child through or truly doesn't understand, finding a way to establish communication with him or her could save your child's life, as it did in this case.

BECOMING YOUR CHILD'S GUARDIAN

Guardianship can best be explained by comparing it to parenting. Parents are effectively the child's guardians by birth or adoption. Parents are responsible for making medical, educational, and life decisions for their children when the children are too young to make competent choices or take care of themselves. When a child becomes legally an adult, she is able to make her own decisions. That means that you can no longer make educational or medical decisions for her.

In the case of a disabled person who becomes an adult but is not able to assume responsibility for himself, the parent must show the court that he is unable to make competent medical and other care decisions without the protection of a guardian. Effectively you ask the court to extend your ability to care for your child by becoming his legal guardian.

It is easy to go with the flow and not deal with this issue. If you haven't changed doctors, most doctors continue to treat your child with your consent as always. When an emergency arises, things can change rapidly. For example, after Billy Ray's emergency room crisis, he ended up on a ventilator for nine days. In order for the ventilator to be removed at my request, guardianship would have to be established. Fortunately, it didn't come to that point, but it is an important thing to remember.

A WORD ABOUT LAWSUITS

The lawsuit issue is something that is always lurking in the background of the relationship between educational or medical professionals and parents. Laws about the rights of disabled children tend to be written in legal jargon that is difficult for professionals and parents to understand. Some rights and privileges may have unclear exceptions. Professionals worry about being sued, and sometimes parents get frustrated and threaten to sue, adding to the professional's worry.

Threatening to sue will only make the relationship more strained. Instead of helping your child as you might intend, it often takes the focus away from that process. Time that could be spent planning for your child gets spent in preparation for a threatened lawsuit. Professionals notify administrators of any threats made, and then they start consultation with attorneys about their liability.

In the event you do have reasonable cause for a lawsuit, you have to look at how it will affect your child's future. In treating a complex child sometimes new approaches and increased risk taking may be required. If you have brought a lawsuit in the past, even if you lost, professionals may be hesitant to take those risks because you might bring suit again.

I know firsthand the frustration parents feel when the rights of their children have been violated or mistakes have been made that will permanently affect their children. We have faced the decision three times in Billy Ray's life.

I will give you an example and tell you why I decided not to sue. The seizures that were caused by a medication reaction have had a permanent impact on Billy Ray. Several of our attorney friends offered to bring suit at reduced fees. I agonized about it and investigated it. I learned that in order to sue the drug company for not listing seizures as a potential side effect, I would probably have to make the psychiatrist, pediatrician, and our HMO parties in the suit because they had prescribed the medication. The pediatrician and psychiatrist were sincere and caring people who tried desperately to help my son and were as devastated by this situation as I was. It did not happen because they were negligent. Unlike the stories you hear of HMOs that won't cover needed treatment or medical testing, our HMO provided Billy Ray with testing and retesting. In my opinion, everything that could have been done to help my son was done.

I had seen cases where families had sued. Afterward, it became difficult for them to get doctors. Educators were cautious about programs for the child after the lawsuit. Children who need extraordinary care cannot succeed with the minimum services allowed them under the law. They need professionals who are willing to be creative. The fear of lawsuits tends to block that creativity. Money gained from winning or settling the lawsuit would not have made things better than a relationship with professionals willing to try harder to help your child.

Thinking through the lawsuit question will have an effect on your personal attitude, even if you do not share your thinking with the professionals involved. It clarifies for you that you are committed to working through problems with the professionals involved with your child.

14

CREATING A COMMUNITY
FOR YOUR CHILD

DISABLED PERSONS have equal access to all public places guaranteed under the Americans with Disabilities Act. We aren't locking all disabled persons away anymore. Yet when I take my son out in public and everyone stares, I find myself looking around and wondering, "Where are his peers?" He is often the only developmentally disabled person we see in restaurants, various types of stores, and even our church.

Taking our complex children out in the community can be hard work. Just getting out the door can be exhausting. If your child is loud or disruptive, the public can be vicious. The question of whether it is worth the bother is always in the forefront.

It is natural to want our disabled children to have the same rights as any other person. I firmly believe Billy Ray has as much right to enjoy all kinds of community outings as anyone. That having been said, it does not guarantee his acceptance in a world that fails to teach the importance of community to everyone.

In recent years, I have become aware that bringing my son into a relationship with his community takes more than being concerned about how he is treated. Although others' discomfort around my son is not my responsibility, it does affect his enjoyment of the event as well. I can either get angry with people for being rude or intolerant, or I can create a system that is more pleasant for us and educate this smaller world to whatever degree possible. When that actually succeeds, it helps the world to see that disabled folks are people who have something to offer.

This problem was not an issue for Billy Ray and me until his medication reaction, at age fourteen, changed him from a quiet child with a charming little smile to a sometimes aggressive, agitated, and noisy person. He still has that smile, but no longer uses it much to win new friends.

When he was little, you could hear a hush overtake our neighborhood restaurant when he would start to speak. He said cute little things that everyone enjoyed. People would let someone else take their places in line for the next table if they thought the table next to Billy Ray was about to open. After the change, people sometimes move away when we are seated next to them. At first, this was humiliating to me.

I have spent years defending Billy Ray and his right to be there. My basic attitude has been it doesn't matter if he is noisy and the party at the next table is trying to have a peaceful conversation. Billy Ray is a child who especially thrives on the stimulation of being out in public. He needs it and so do I.

One of our former caregiving assistants said that we should stop taking him out to restaurants and grocery stores. After all, the other guests in a restaurant are paying customers too. I was outraged at the very thought of keeping him locked up at home. Although I certainly understand why some parents decide it is too much frustration to take their children out in public, I think Billy Ray actually deteriorates with the isolation. The first words out of his mouth every morning are, "Where we going?"

When the outrage I felt at her suggestion subsided, I did see what the caregiver meant. It is not pleasant to dine with so much noise coming from neighboring tables that you cannot relax to have a conversation with your dinner partners. I wanted Billy Ray to have the community outings he needs and deserves, but I wanted to find a way to provide his needs without totally alienating others.

DINING OUT IN RESTAURANTS

Drive-up windows are not satisfactory to Billy Ray. He wants "restaurant." He remembers the sense of community he felt in our little neighborhood restaurant when he was younger.

My late husband spent a lot of time in the hospital the last few years of his life. I picked up Billy Ray from day care after work and we went to visit Daddy every night. If we went directly home to prepare dinner, we were interrupted with telephone calls. Screening calls was upsetting to Billy Ray because he would hear the telephone ring. When the telephone rang it meant we should answer it. I couldn't just unplug it because of my business. Thus, a ritual of going to Robbie's Restaurant most nights began. Eventually I got an answering service so we did not need to go to Robbie's every night, but Billy Ray loved it so much we still went often.

He longs for that sense of community and enjoyment. We set about creating a community for our family. Frequenting the same places regularly gives your child and the staff there a chance to know each other.

When waiters and waitresses get to know Billy Ray, some will take an interest in him and attempt to meet his needs. They will bring his soft drink with his menu and get to know how Billy Ray likes things. Consequently, he is quieter and we all enjoy the time more. I make it a point to let these servers know, both by verbal appreciation and a little more in the tip (when I can), that their extra efforts made Billy Ray's experience more pleasant for all. This is rewarding for them. Usually they make even more effort in future visits. We ask for the same server whenever we come in. After we know that server awhile, we ask about his or her schedule and avoid going to the restaurant on the server's nights off if possible.

Your family undoubtedly enjoys different kinds of foods. Cultivate two or three restaurants that you can choose from and work with those restaurants toward establishing a community relationship for your family. In addition, have some variety of choices, so you can go to another restaurant if you decide to go out on your special server's night off. Make an effort to get to know the management in each of your restaurant choices. The managers usually will come through for you.

The Red Lobster chain is a good example. Although we don't go to their restaurants that often, we like to go on special occasions. They have made family gatherings that could have been difficult with Billy Ray pleasant for us. One of their restaurants is in the city where my husband's parents live. When we have a family birthday or some of Larry's adult children and grandchildren are in town, I telephone the manager at that Red Lobster. I make reservations and remind her of who we are and what our needs are. They do not normally take reservations but will for us. She knows that Billy Ray can't tolerate waiting and that if he gets their wonderful cheese-and-herb biscuits and raspberry lemonade right away, it will help to occupy him until his food arrives. She assigns a top-notch server to us and instructs him or her on our needs. Because of this supportive approach, Billy Ray is able to remain calmer and others in the family are able to enjoy visiting with each other. I make it a point to call the manager the following day and thank her.

Despite all the attempts to keep things moving and the special work on the part of the servers, there are times that Billy Ray is just noisy and unfocused for no apparent reason. When we frequent the same places regularly, they know that this is not the norm and they are more accepting of him.

WHEN PEOPLE STARE

Stares from strangers really used to bother me. I took them personally. I am ashamed at how often I used to say, "Didn't your mother teach you not to stare?" Now, whenever possible, I try to catch the eyes of people staring at my son. I smile instead of glare. If they are close enough to engage in conversation, I will sometimes introduce Billy Ray to folks. Other times, as we pass by someone who has glared at him, I will say, "I wish we could have been quieter," or "Autism is a difficult thing." I don't apologize for Billy Ray being who he is, but I am sincere in regretting if he disturbs anyone.

At one point, I thought that children's staring and ridiculing Billy

Ray was because of the attitude of their parents. After watching the children who make fun or stare, I now think it appears to be more like a lack of attention from their parents rather than bias passed from parent to child. It appears often to be fear on the part of the child. For some, the situation is just strange because Billy Ray is different.

When a child stares at Billy Ray for several minutes and smiling does not change that, I sometimes approach the parent and ask if I could explain to his or her child that Billy Ray is not going to hurt them, that he can't control the noise and isn't being naughty. We then have often observed major changes in the expression of the child. We introduce Billy Ray, he waves, and the child relaxes. Some parents have thanked me, stating they did not realize their children might be afraid.

SHOPPING IN STORES

Various kinds of stores can be handled similarly to restaurants. Choose the ones that work for your child because they don't have whatever tempts your child—with Billy Ray, it is soda pop—at the end of every aisle. Choose a clerk who is friendly to your child and reasonably fast in providing service. Make it a point to learn the clerk's name, and then call the clerk by name. I encourage Billy Ray to greet them too, and I call Billy Ray by his name so the clerk learns his name. This way, you teach your child social skills but also help him to be more accepted. If your child is nonverbal, cue him to wave or smile.

Be sure to meet and thank the store manager for the way the staff accommodates you. This eases shopping pressures when your child has episodes of negative behaviors or makes noise in the store. The relationship brings the added benefit of making the manager more willing to order special foods or products your child may need.

If your child has unusual proportions for his size, you need a relationship with clothing stores. It is difficult to shop with a child who will want everything whether it is his size or not. Yet, you really need to have him try things on because once you bring them home, it may be difficult to get the items away from him to return them. Your child may not understand why a store fails to have something that he wants in his size. The scene that occurs is uncomfortable for all concerned.

If you find a clerk or clothing manager who understands the situation, you can call first. He or she will usually check the racks for the size and type of item you want. You can arrange to bring your child in to try those items on or, if you know they are the right size, just pick them up. Sometimes that doesn't satisfy Billy Ray. He wants to "shop." The clerk will at least ensure that there is what we need on the rack before we come into the store.

OTHER TYPES OF BUSINESSES

Make a list of the types of businesses your family needs to frequent, including those providing leisure activities. If you enjoy bowling or miniature golf, for example, establish a relationship with the manager. Share your family's needs and ask for whatever accommodations you need.

Barbers and beauticians can be especially challenging. You need to find someone who is patient enough to deal with your child if she is noisy or wiggles a lot. You also have to find someone who will cut your child's hair the way she is most comfortable with. The barber may need to cut your child's hair the same way every time to keep your child happy. If your child is like Billy Ray, he or she is not interested in changing the way things are done.

We use the same feed store for horse grain and dog food. They know us so well that Billy Ray and his caregiver could go to pick up needed items. This was a store without attractive nuisances, so Billy Ray could enjoy going in, giving the clerk his list, and paying the bill with the check we sent. It gives him a sense of responsibility for his animals.

BECOMING PART OF THE COMMUNITY

Most disabled children are able to give something to the community. When classroom settings no longer worked for him, the special-education director and I arranged for Billy Ray to do small volunteer jobs with his educational assistant. The community got to know him because they saw him putting away shopping carts from the parking lot at the local grocer.

When he went to a popular restaurant for lunch, people could remember him from the grocery store.

Think about the tasks your child is capable of doing that will benefit some organization. Billy Ray is doing cleaning projects in our church. It gives him a sense of accomplishment and is helpful to the church.

Because of my years as a guardian, Billy Ray has visited elderly people since he was a young child. His attention span for long visits is no longer there. However, he can deliver meals on wheels, carry the meal to the door, and brighten someone's day. It gives meaning to his life as well as to the elderly people on his route.

Establishing relationships within his community is more difficult, but once established, they can be some of the most meaningful. You should realize that understanding your child takes some effort for others.

When we were looking for a church in our new community, I telephoned several pastors to find out if they met our needs. Music has a calming effect on Billy Ray, which makes it easier for him to sit through the sermon. There are still times that he speaks out. When I called one pastor and explained the situation he said, "Have you considered attending without him?" Because of that question, we almost passed on that church. Billy Ray and the Reverend Ray Jones would have missed what became a special relationship for six years. It took a while for the church to get used to his sudden noise; it undoubtedly frightened some other churchgoers for a while. Billy Ray became an important part of that church community because the people took the time to get to know and love him.

If you are able to get respite-care services, have the caregivers do meaningful activities with your child rather than watch movies or kill time. Plan community activities they can do together. It could be anything that your child is able to do, from visiting seniors in a nursing home, to picking up garbage in the local park, to petting animals at the Humane Society. Participating in activities your child is interested in will add meaning to your child's life. In addition to the sense of him giving something to the community, you may work out career opportunities down the road. Engaging your child in various volunteer activities gives you the chance to see if there is something that really motivates him.

It is simpler to stay home than to create a community for your child, but your child, your family, and the community will lose the benefits of the relationships you can build. Make your world as small and warm as you need it to be, but build community relationships to give your child a sense of belonging to a world beyond his family. Your child has as much to give the world as it has to give to your child.

CHAPTER

15

HIRING, TRAINING, AND SUPERVISING CAREGIVERS

WITH A COMPLEX CHILD, having some kind of in-home assistance may be a necessity for you and your family. There are many factors and questions to consider in employing someone to help you care for your child. This chapter will present an overview of the most important ones, along with some of my own experiences.

Depending on your child's diagnosis, needs, and the area in which you live, there may be funding available for in-home help. This can range from a few hours of respite care each month to a full-time caregiver. Some programs are federally funded but administered through state or county programs, and some have matching funding between federal and local programs. Contact your local agency for developmental disabilities or your county health department to find out about funding that might be available for in-home support staff.

A key factor in determining whether your child receives in-home services is generally whether you would need to place him out of the home without such services. For the most part, if providing in-home support is cheaper for the government than placement, or if there is no appropriate placement, it is more likely to provide support.

Some programs find, train, and place caregivers with you and supervise them as well. Most provide funding and expect you to be the employer and supervisor. Finding appropriate caregivers and keeping them can be more of a challenge than taking care of your complex child.

HAVING AN EMPLOYEE IN YOUR HOME

I have supervised employees in various settings over the years. There is a difference when you have an employee in your own home, especially if the person is paid by a third party. If an employee comes into your home, it is natural to treat him or her as part of the family. That is a comfortable and even somewhat healthy situation for your child.

However, once you have crossed the line between employee in the home and part of the family, performance and dependability may begin to change. The pressure to perform at home is often less than in a workplace outside of a home. Family is expected to understand more than supervisors are. You can lose a great deal of your authority.

Employees who are paid by governmental agencies may assume the boss is the agency and the parents are their friends. Although both you and the agency personnel may explain that the parent is supervisor, the employee may believe that the agency providing the paycheck is boss. For example, tardiness can be a problem. If caregivers see you as friend, they do not expect you to monitor their attendance even though you are responsible for signing their time slips.

If you do not work outside of your home, whether you work at home or not, you are expected to be available for socializing. You must monitor the situation closely in the beginning to avoid becoming too involved in the caregiver's personal life. You must be firm about needing time to work while you have help.

The "dumb-parent treatment" is just as real in the employer-employee relationship as in other settings. In the example I gave in chapter 10 of the caregiver who changed the sequence of Billy Ray's bath, it became clear that she didn't respect my authority. In the beginning of her employment, she was given time to read the written caregiver's manual. During a lengthy pre-employment interview, I had told her that I had written the caregiver's manual. I actually revised it after she started working. Additionally, I demonstrated the procedures and personally trained her for two weeks before I left her alone with my son.

At the time, we had a behavior therapist coming into the home for one hour a week as a consultant. To my amazement, after Billy Ray had been agitated at bath time for three weekends and the caregiver said nothing was different, she told the consultant, "Oh by the way I changed the sequence of YOUR schedule for Billy Ray's bath. It works a lot better." She assumed the consultant designed the program and was the boss. In addition to her lack of respect for my authority, this demonstrated a lack of attention to detail and poor listening skills, because the manual explained the need for consistency in the sequence of steps in activities. I had personally explained it to her before and after her employment began.

With all this to consider, you may wonder whether it is worth it. I have been there many times. The reality is that if your child requires one-on-one supervision, sometimes on a twenty-four-hour basis, and her care is exhausting, you need help. You can live sleep deprived for only so long. Your marriage could be damaged by an inability to communicate with each other. If you have other children, you may not be able to meet their needs without help with your complex child. It is difficult to take care of your own medical and dental needs let alone get a haircut occasionally without help. You can work through the difficulty of having in-home staff if you stay on top of the major issues, preventing as many problems as possible before they occur. Be clear about expectations from the initial interview.

Before you interview your first applicant, be clear on the details with the source of the funding. Clarify who will be responsible for employee supervision and what responsibilities are expected of you. Ask about any rules you need to be aware of that could affect your child's eligibility for services. Examples of this would be reporting hours worked and any obligation to provide meals for staff.

In our particular situation, the county pays the salary when we have staff, but we are considered the employer. Employee hiring, firing, training, and supervision are our obligation. We are to approve time slips before they are sent to the broker that the county retains to take care of payroll.

No workplace is free of employee problem areas. Attendance problems, theft, dishonesty, and alcoholism or drug use are things we hear about in most workplaces. In your home, those same employee problems are more difficult to deal with. For example, in an average workplace, if someone calls in sick, other employees have to bear the extra load. If a caregiver calls in sick, there is usually no backup but the parent. If you are a single parent, or both parents work outside of the home, a caregiver who has poor attendance may affect your ability to maintain employment. Employee problems can affect the family's finances as well. If a parent must stay home with the child because the caregiver fails to show up, the parent's earnings may suffer, especially if it is time without pay. Minor theft, such as taking food from a family struggling to make ends meet, can have a major impact on the family budget.

NAVIGATING THE HIRING PROCESS

You have to be very professional about the entire caregiver situation from the start. I recommend starting with the steps I've outlined below.

Determine What You Need

Decide what characteristics and skills you need in a caregiver. Do you want an experienced person, or would you prefer someone who is more easily trained by you?

The degree of your child's complexities makes a big difference in the skill level you seek. If your child's behavior and diagnoses are complicated, experienced caregivers may actually be harder to train than caregivers with no experience but a great attitude. Sometimes experienced caregivers may be more likely to do things their own way than listen to the parent as supervisor. If your child needs consistency or a specific sequence of activities, she can be negatively affected by this kind of deviation from what is expected. Your child is also affected by the strain this puts on your relationship with the employee.

The flip side is that someone who has never worked with a disabled child will not necessarily understand your child's behavior. The caregiver may see it as spoiled-child syndrome. It is pretty hard to explain to the uninitiated what it is like to have a child throw something across the room, missing their head by inches, or to watch a teenager throw himself on the floor in frustration.

Write a Job Description

Be specific about qualifications and responsibilities. I try to make it clear why certain qualifications are important. For example, if steps in Billy Ray's routine are done out of sequence, it can confuse him and result in negative behavior, including aggression. That is more detail than you would normally see in a job description, but it gives you a chance to discuss the importance of those qualifications in a job interview.

Write a Caregiver Manual

The manual should have information about your child's needs, schedule, and procedures. It should also include expectations and house rules. It must be specific. Expecting someone to use his or her common sense can backfire on you. If something is written in the manual, you can refer employees back to it for review.

Whether you work at home or outside of the home, you want employees to be able to find answers to their questions without having to ask you repeatedly. It is easier for them to ask you how to do things than to go to the manual. However, the constant interruptions for questions covered by the manual are an annoyance and can create problems in your ability to do your work. The manual minimizes the employee's need to call you, but only if the employee actually uses it. I explain to employees that I want them to ask me about things that are unclear, but I expect them to look in the manual first.

Manuals do not need to be fancy. Sometimes the agency that assists

with funding can provide you a fill-in-the-blank form that you can supplement with additional items you want included. I started out using
those types of forms until I developed a manual that worked best in our
situation. A partial sample of the caregiver's manual I used when we had
a full-time employee is available on my website, www.parentingyourcom
plexchild.com.

Revisions will undoubtedly be necessary. When you make changes
during the employment of an existing caregiver, I suggest you write a
memo to the employee referring him to the revised section of the manual
and asking him to initial the memo when he has reviewed the revisions.

At the back of the manual, I include copies of helpful articles about
Billy Ray's disabilities. For example, Billy Ray experiences symptoms of
autism, Down syndrome, and bipolar disorder. There are many useful
articles on the Web and elsewhere that help to explain why he might
need certain things or respond in certain ways. I would not provide a
book on autism or other diagnoses Billy Ray experiences, because he is
unique. I include only articles that are relevant to him individually. During times when Billy Ray is taking an unexpected nap or watching a
movie, we expect employees to review the manual and attached articles
rather than bring a book from home to read.

Employees have frequently asked to take the manual home, where
they feel they can review it better. This can be a mistake. We have lost
manuals in this way. In addition, our manuals contain private, personal
information about Billy Ray and the family.

During the training phase, I work out time for employees to spend
reading the manual. I demonstrate the procedures, asking them to follow
along in the manual. Later I back off and ask them to complete activities
following the manual guidelines, but remain available for questions.
Eventually they do not need to refer to the manual for routine activities.
I find that when they follow the manual they remember more than if
they come into my office to ask me how to do a procedure.

Plan the Recruiting Process

Talk to the funding agency about any assistance they may offer in recruiting staff. Sometimes they are able to refer applicants for your consider-

ation. Sometimes they are not involved in the recruitment process other than providing forms for the criminal-history clearance or payroll forms.

Recruiting applicants through referrals from friends, churches, support groups, etc. is more likely to bring the best applicants. I have prepared flyers to leave in church foyers, agency waiting rooms, etc. Unfortunately, I have not had great response from those efforts.

The applicant pool available through newspaper advertising can be less desirable. Legal rules relative to reference checks make verifying an applicant's qualifications difficult. For the most part, the only questions former employers will answer pertain to the length of employment and whether they would rehire the employee. If an employee is fired, even for cause, the former employer risks liability for disclosing that fact to prospective employers.

When you write a newspaper ad, be as specific about the qualifications as possible. Here is a sample of an advertisement I wrote for a caregiver for Billy Ray. It is longer than the average ad, but I hoped to weed out some applicants. For example, applicants who don't want to bathe a twenty-year-old will not call.

> Looking for special personality who will bring the right mix of humor, patience, flexibility, attention to detail, great listening skills, high energy, and commitment to be a buddy and caregiver for twenty-year-old mentally and behaviorally challenged man. Attitude, flexibility, and dependability more important than experience. Must be willing to try new methods and procedures to meet client's needs. Must be willing to deal with hygiene assistance to client, including bathing. References should demonstrate good listening skills, attitude, and dependability. Good driving record and criminal-history check required.

Note that no specific diagnosis is included. Billy Ray's primary diagnosis is Down syndrome. Many people think that Down syndrome people are all sweetness and easy to take care of. Some are, but Billy Ray is not. I like to say that Down syndrome is the least of his problems. Placing diagnoses in the ad brings stereotyping and unrealistic expectations.

The wording in your ad will make a difference in the number of calls you receive. For example, we used to live on a small farm. When I put a line in an ad that said staff would assist Billy Ray with some farm chores such as feeding horses, I got over 100 calls. Most of the callers had no real desire to work with a disabled young man; they just wanted to work on a farm or with the horses.

Prepare for the Interview

I like to prepare two lists of questions for potential applicants. The first one consists of questions I want to ask respondents when they call. This helps screen applicants so that you interview only the most desirable candidates. The interview process is difficult to involve Billy Ray in, and finding care in order to conduct lots of interviews is also a problem. Screening the applicants on the phone reduces the number of actual interviews. For example, I always ask questions right away about their comfort with assisting Billy Ray with hygiene and toileting. Occasionally it will be clear, either from what they say or their hesitance in responding, that this is not going to be something they can handle. There is no reason to spend time preparing for and conducting an interview if they can't handle those tasks.

The second list is questions for the actual interview. You would choose these questions based on the things that are most important to you and your child. I ask hard questions about dependability, including tardiness in their past employment. Billy Ray may not tell time, but his inner clock knows when someone is late. Therefore, dependability is an important issue.

It is helpful to leave space on the lists so I can take notes on their responses. I make copies so that I can reuse the forms.

Select the Employee

You will get a good idea which candidate you like best in the in-person interview. However, I don't recommend you offer the job to anyone at this point.

Occasionally you will have additional thoughts when looking over your notes, or there will be a red flag in the reference check. As stated above, former employers risk legal liability for sharing detrimental information about applicants. However, I have found that former employers will give important hints when they find out the job you are hiring for involves caring for a disabled person. One former employer said to me,

"You know I can't tell you negatives, even if there is something I think you should know," several times in a brief conversation. I finally said to her, "You have said that to me three or four times; should I take that as a red flag?" She responded that she would.

You might anticipate many applicants, especially if jobs are scarce, but that is just not the reality. As stated, one time I put in the ad that part of the job was assisting Billy Ray with farm chores, including feeding the horses. I got over a hundred responses to that ad, but interviewed only five people. Because I have made the ad more specific, I get fewer calls. Unfortunately, my experience has been that some people feel this work is beneath them, and a large percentage of the applicants think it will be an easy job.

My standards for employees have changed over the years. I used to be concerned about the appearance of an employee. Employees often take Billy Ray to medical and school appointments or out in the community. The appearance of an employee can be a reflection on how Billy Ray is cared for. On the other hand, we had a twenty-year-old man working with Billy Ray who would come in white Dockers pants, nice shirts, and fancy shoes. He made a great impression at medical and school appearances, but he was afraid of getting dirty when he helped Billy Ray with his farm chores.

Our most unusual hire occurred because Billy Ray reached out to someone whom I probably would not have hired in the normal recruitment process. Benjamin was referred to us to do some short-term farm chores. Some mornings, it was pretty obvious he had done a bit of partying the night before. Nevertheless he worked hard on the farm, which fascinated Billy Ray. Billy Ray wanted to be outside with Benjamin constantly and was really drawn to him.

At the time we hired Benjamin to do the outside work, we were employing the young man who showed up in fancy clothing and didn't want to get dirty. He would take Billy Ray out to see Benjamin and then sort of disappear back in the house. Not knowing Benjamin well, I was frightened by that.

During the time Benjamin was working on the farm, the caregiver left our employment. Billy Ray is very upset when caregivers do not come to work and is generally devastated when their employment terminates. This time Billy Ray never asked about the departed staff. He wanted to be outside with Benjamin and was determined that Benjamin should be his caregiver.

Billy Ray's plan to make Benjamin his caregiver seemed an unlikely plan. However, as I was contemplating another recruitment process, I began to notice improved interest in life and improved self-esteem on the part of both men. Billy Ray and Benjamin were good for each other. Based on that observation, I made the decision to invest the extra training time it would take with Benjamin.

Benjamin is probably the most successful employee we have ever had in terms of the way he relates to Billy Ray. Although he no longer works for us full-time, Benjamin is the person I trust most with Billy Ray, other than my husband. Fortunately, he is still available on occasion for evenings or special events Larry and I need to attend.

Turnover is inevitable with caregivers, but very stressful for your child and for you. According to our fiduciary, who acts as broker to receive county funds and issues payroll to employees, six months is now considered long-term employment for a caregiver. The fiduciary told me that we retain employees longer than most families. Our longest-term employee, Benjamin, worked for us approximately one year.

We have thought about and talked about why things worked so well with Benjamin. I don't think we will ever know for sure, but here are some thoughts that might give you insight in selecting employees:

- The personality match between Billy Ray and Benjamin was special. Both of them grew as a result of their time together.
- Benjamin had no experience other than being a Dad. He had no preconceived notions about how Billy Ray should be.
- Benjamin was able to see assisting Billy Ray with hygiene in the same way as he did caring for his own children when they were little.
- Benjamin was proud of his achievement and Billy Ray's achievement.
- Benjamin became Billy Ray's buddy and felt comfortable in our home, but took supervision well.
- Benjamin took his job seriously.

It took work to train someone with so little experience. The benefit to Billy Ray of that special relationship made the extra work worth it. I am not sure how many more Benjamins there are out there, but look for one.

Train and Supervise Your Employee

As mentioned above, the manual is an important part of the training. You want staff to be able to find answers quickly even when you are not available. They will be more consistent if they follow the manual rather than wait to ask questions. Encourage them to use the manual.

The activity visuals that I created to train Billy Ray to do activities and establish a sequence he was comfortable with have become great training tools for caregivers. In fact, I have made them on occasion more for the assistant than for Billy Ray.

The applicant pool often includes people from other cultures who may not have total command of English. Maybe an employee speaks reasonably good English but doesn't read well. The visuals help in that regard. Additionally, I was shocked to discover that some caregivers do not do simple tasks, such as dish washing, mopping a floor, or making simple breakfasts in ways that I would have expected everyone to understand. I found it necessary to do an activity visual for use by one employee who was helping Billy Ray mop his bathroom floor. The employee saw the visual as being for Billy Ray's benefit, but he got the message about the steps involved, such as using clean water daily, not just changing it once a week.

Do periodic written and oral performance appraisals. If caregivers are doing well, this gives you a chance to praise them. If things are not going well, it allows you to deal with problem areas before they get too far out of hand.

As I've repeated throughout this book, each complex child is a unique individual with specific habits, needs, skills, and abilities. Matching a caregiver to your child can be a difficult and sometimes frustrating process. But it can be well worth the time and effort—for you, your family, and your child—when you find the right one.

CHAPTER 16

MAPPING THE JOURNEY

I ONCE HAD A CHEAP PRINT hanging in my office that said, "Life Is a Journey, Not a Destination." As with any journey, there are detours along the way. Plans have to be changed. It is impossible to plan for every circumstance.

As stated earlier, when Billy Ray was a toddler, we pressed the pediatrician to predict what level he would function at as an adult. We had to make a choice between therapy that wasn't covered by insurance and the payments we were making on life insurance to fund a trust we had created for him. Given the way he was blooming developmentally, we agreed with the doctor that he would likely be able to function in some kind of semi-independent living program.

The transition plan I created for my son, while we were waiting to see if he would return to what was normal for him before he experienced the seizures, had goals that are no longer totally appropriate. At twenty-three years old, the dream for him has totally changed because he will always need a high degree of supervision. Additionally, he has now been in two different types of short-term placements, and we are able to see that he would not fit in well in a group setting.

The fear of what will happen to your child after you are no longer available to him is a pressure on your heart that is always there. I hope that you and your child have a lot of life together before that point. You can take comfort in the things that you can do now to protect your child even after you are no longer together. If you make plans now for that event and stay consistent in yearly preparations, you are free to deal with your child's present life without as much anxiety about the future. You will know that you have done all that you can for his future.

Goals and planning for your child are important. However, flexibility and lots of backup planning are just as important, given the changes in circumstances experienced not only by your child, but also by those you felt certain would always be there for your child if you were no longer available.

Although this chapter involves estate planning for disabled children, I am leaving specifics about wills and trusts to your local attorney and to the many books on that topic. I thought it would be more beneficial to you, the reader, for me to share my experience as a professional fiduciary (guardian, conservator, and/or trustee) in trying to carry out those estate plans.

CHOOSING SOMEONE TO CARE FOR YOUR CHILD

Estate planning documents, such as wills and trusts, generally nominate someone as guardian, conservator, or trustee to provide the level of support or care your child will need in case of your death or disability. The terms may mean different things in different areas. For example, in some states the person who is in charge of the financial assets of someone else might be called a "conservator," and in other states the person might be called the "guardian of the estate." Check with your attorney about the laws in your area.

This person might be a member of your family, a friend, or a professional. In some cases, your child (even though he may be an adult by then) will actually live with the guardian, especially if the nominee is a family member or friend. A professional guardian will generally place the child in a suitable living arrangement and supervise the situation to ensure his care and needs are met.

Often, you will choose more than one person—a married couple, for example. Needless to say, you should give a good deal of careful consideration to choosing someone to care for your child. You should discuss the situation with that person and get the person's approval before putting his or her name in the documents.

Even when choosing family members or friends, you need people who are responsible and trustworthy, levelheaded, loving, and caring. It's probably a good thing if they are parents, although they still may not be prepared for the challenge of a complex child. Hopefully, they know your child and have had some experience in dealing with her. You also want someone who will be able to provide your child with stability—your sister may be a wonderful person with a supportive spouse, but her job may require that she transfer to new locations every couple of years.

In some cases, you will designate a professional who is not a friend or family member. Such people may offer a level of expertise you cannot expect from a layperson; they will know the legal issues and the system and be able to ensure your child has access to certain programs. However, in all likelihood the professional will not have the kind of personal knowledge of your child that a family member or friend would. The information you maintain will be important to the professional's ability to make informed decisions for your child.

Even the most considerate planning for your child and his or her representatives has a way of being changed by the circumstances of life. Maybe your youngest brother and sister-in-law seem to be the perfect guardians for your child at the time you do your estate plan. Here are a few things that might affect that nomination down the road:

- Your brother and his wife divorce and he marries someone who would not be willing or able to deal with your child in the way your first sister-in-law would have.

- God forbid they are killed in a car wreck with you.

- Health problems in their own family prevent them from taking on the responsibility of your child.

- They move to another area of the country. They are still willing to take on the responsibility, but do not really know your child anymore or have the faintest idea how to best take care of him.

- The court finds your nominee to be an unfit person to be appointed guardian or other designation for your child because of some problems that you were unable to anticipate.

- Maybe your nominee simply no longer feels he (they) are able to take on the responsibility.

In all of these situations, a stranger approved by the court—not your brother and his wife—could end up being responsible for your child's care.

I have seen estate planning documents specify that the same standard of living the child received in the parent's lifetime should be maintained, but then fail to demonstrate what that standard is. If the professional or distant friend or family member designated to act on behalf of the child did not have a high degree of communication with you and your child, he or she may not have a clear understanding of what that standard of living was. Sometimes parents have not provided the child's chosen representative with this kind of information because they have died suddenly or they suffer from a physical condition, such as dementia. Key issues such as medical history and even funeral planning for the child are not always known to your child's representative after you are no longer available.

GETTING IT RIGHT

I recommend that you do as much of the following four steps as you are able to do:

1. See your attorney and create a plan with as many alternate nominees as she recommends for guardian, conservator, or trustee.

2. Keep relevant information about your child with your estate planning documents. If you keep your estate planning documents in a safe deposit box, include only a letter to your child's representative and a copy of the abbreviated medical history discussed in chapter 12, a

sample of which is shown in appendix figure 8. (Both the letter and the medical history should be revised and replaced every year around some easily remembered date, such as your child's birthday.) In the letter, tell your child's representative where you keep information on your child. If you keep copies of your estate planning documents at home or with other business papers, maintain a file or notebook containing your child's information right there with the other important documents. I will give you some ideas of what to place in the file in the "Providing Essential Information" section below.

3. Ask your attorney to maintain a copy of the letter and abbreviated medical history in her file for you. Send her revised copies every year and provide her with any changes in contact information for your child's nominated representatives. That might be a good time to review those nominations. Consider whether nominations seem as appropriate as they did at the time you drew up the documents. If not, your attorney can advise you about making changes.

4. Have a discussion or correspondence with nominees concerning your child at least once a year. Provide them with a copy of the revised letter and medical history. Give them time to review it and formulate any questions they might have before you have a conversation with them. This enables them to ask questions while you are able to answer.

WRITING EVERYTHING DOWN

Much of the information you want to provide your child's representative is already available if you are following the documentation system recommended in chapter 12. If you are already revising the abbreviated history, medical and otherwise, it will be useful in this situation as well.

No matter how close the nominated representative is to your family, do not assume that the person will know where you keep things or be familiar with pertinent medical information relative to your child. Here is a story from our journey as an example:

When Billy Ray came to us at fifteen months, my late husband had no experience with Down syndrome children. He was sure that the almond-shaped eyes common to Down syndrome were crossed eyes and that Billy Ray needed surgery. He mentioned it so many times, I finally brought it up to the pediatrician. Because Billy Ray had had surgery for tear-duct issues prior to his to adoptive placement, she suggested I have Raymond take Billy Ray to see an ophthalmologist. This was a needed follow-up anyway, and Raymond could talk to the doctor about Billy Ray's eyes. Raymond did take Billy Ray for his appointment and the doctor was able to reassure him that Billy Ray was not cross-eyed. From that point on, Raymond alone took our son for his annual eye checkups.

Raymond would tell me about what the doctor said about Billy Ray's need for glasses and relate cute little things that he did in the doctor's office. He never mentioned any additional problems with Billy Ray's eyes. Following his father's death, I took Billy Ray for his yearly appointment at twelve years old. The doctor said, "The cataracts are getting a little cloudier." Of course, my response was, "What cataracts?" Raymond went to his grave without telling me that they were monitoring Billy Ray yearly for pin-size cataracts that would someday have to be removed. Whether he thought he had told me and hadn't, or just didn't think it was important until the doctor wanted to do something, I don't know. But it certainly came as a big shock to learn this information almost a year following Raymond's death, when I could no longer ask him about it.

If your child's representative is one of your other children or a close friend, it is entirely possible that information about your child either wasn't communicated or was forgotten. Maintaining the information in writing as you go along eliminates this problem and ensures that you will not forget it later as well.

PROVIDING ESSENTIAL INFORMATION

For the file you maintain with your estate planning documents, I would suggest including two types of information:

1. A memorandum to the representative including the following points and answering the following questions, whether you think the representative already knows the information or not:

    • Introduce your child as a person. Describe his personality to the degree you can put a description into words. Some examples of cute things that he does or even some negative behaviors might help. Include things like nicknames your child is called and has for others in the family.

- What are his joys and what are his fears to the degree you know them? What is he most proud of and what bothers him most?

- Discuss his strengths and weaknesses and his needs. You may even include reference to the visuals you have created.

- What is his relationship with certain other individuals? (Provide contact information.) Is there any relationship that would be unhealthy for him to continue? Or are there some worth pursuing?

- What are his regular activities, including vocational, educational, recreational, and church involvement?

- What plans do you have for your child? What are his dreams, whether they seem logical to you or not?

- What educational or vocational training has he had? What opportunities might he have to use that training?

- What government programs have you looked into or are aware of as options for your child?

- Note any recommendations that you may have for helping him adjust to losing you.

2. A basic fact sheet with general information about your child:

    - Full name.

    - Date and place of birth.

    - Social Security number and other identifying information.

    - The names, birthdates, and general identifying information about you and your child's other parent, even if the other parent is not alive when writing this information.

    - Contact information for doctors, therapists, case managers, and any other professional involved in the child's life and care.

    - Location of history files, such as the documents you are currently maintaining for professionals.

- Any family medical history you are aware of on a separate sheet or at least a paragraph in the memo. Sometimes medical professionals will inquire about a patient's family history of cancer, diabetes, or other conditions. It is important to have that information. If the child is adopted, provide what you may know of his family history.

- Benefits the child receives based on his disability or other factors, including any benefits he may be able to receive as a result of your death.

- Funeral trusts or arrangements made for your child. If no arrangements have been made, you might wish to include your own wishes and any preferences you know your child might have.

Each year you can do a brief letter to the representative with a copy to your attorney for the file and one for your files. This letter is an update on what has happened with the child the previous year—sort of like your child were writing a Christmas letter to his friends, but with more detail. If goals you have for your child have changed based on circumstances that have occurred, list those. If medication, conditions, or doctors have changed, list those too. Alternatively, you could just do this yearly letter for your file only and send a note about where the file is located to both the lawyer and the representative. You also should remember to verify the representative's contact information and update it for the attorney each year.

GOING FORWARD

Try to live in the present to the degree that you are able. Concentrate on what you can change, not what you cannot change or even anticipate. Give your child the highest degree of independence and quality of life you can. The more independence she can achieve in your lifetime, the less dependent she will be when you are no longer able to take care of her.

The communication and documentation systems suggested in this book will teach someone to take care of your child if you are hit by a car.

As I was finishing this chapter, I thought about the parents of the clients whom I worked with. Many of the parents' estate plans made provisions "to enable him to maintain the same standard of living he enjoyed during my lifetime." What does that mean? Take him out for dinner at a favorite buffet? If so, what were his favorite foods? In many cases, the child can't communicate that to his or her new guardian. I once did an activity visual I created for Billy Ray to understand the steps in going to a buffet restaurant. It also has a list of his favorite foods, so that anyone taking him to that buffet would know what he normally likes. These same types of visuals that you do for your child in the present are great tools for an estate planning file as well.

As you are working to make your child's life as meaningful as possible, be reassured that the documentation you use for her today is also preparing for the future.

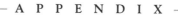

APPENDIX

THIS APPENDIX PROVIDES SAMPLES of some of the documentation and visuals I have used. You can adapt any or all of them to what works for your child. There are other samples on my website www.parentingyourcomplexchild .com.

Sample Visuals

- Communication (picture) planners
- Activity visuals
- Picture schedules

Sample Documents

- Routine tracking forms
- Summary forms
- Abbreviated history of development, behavior, and treatment
- Task list
- Sample comparison of functioning at various points
- Transitional plan

SAMPLE VISUALS

Visuals can be used in many different ways in combination with each other or individually. Adapt them to what works best for your child.

Communication Planners

Appendix figure 1 is a sample of one of Billy Ray's first planners with communication symbols. After several years of using the system, they look more professional than displayed here. I decided to use this picture because I wanted you to see that they do not need to be perfect. The main thing is whether they communicate to your child what you want him to understand. This picture shows a combination of symbols made using Boardmaker software and from the digital pictures I have taken. If you use digital pictures, try to trim everything out of the picture other than your child doing the activity.

There are other ways to make the symbols, I am sure. I insert the pictures into a Microsoft Word document and size the picture. Then I insert a written cue in a small textbox on the picture. The easiest and most economical way is to put as many symbols on a page as you can. It saves paper as well as laminating sheets. It also saves a lot of time.

Note that symbols can be made to whatever size your child sees well and can handle (when removing from the page) best. In Billy Ray's case, a three-inch square works best because he doesn't see well. If your child has no vision issues, a two-inch square might work fine and be less bulky.

Experiment also with the background color if you use software symbols instead of digital pictures. The vision specialist told me that for Billy Ray a yellow background with heavy black lines outlining the symbols made it easier for him to see. Use whatever your child is most able to see.

I prefer printing on glossy paper because the symbols are clearer and it is thick enough to give them some stability. The cost of glossy paper varies greatly,

APPENDIX FIGURE 1   Sample planner.

so shop around. For example, we can buy a package of 100 sheets at Costco. The same brand in some other stores may be priced the same, but contain less than half the number of sheets. In one store, the same brand of glossy paper was five dollars more than the Costco price for half the number of sheets.

The pages are then laminated and cut apart. Small pieces of Velcro are attached to the back of each symbol. You may have to buy your own laminating machine or ask your developmental disabilities case manager to help you find a source that will provide you with one or at least laminate your sheets for you. Check with the photocopy businesses in your area. Some may have laminating machines you can use or will do it for you. If you use glossy paper, you could skip the laminating temporarily. We did that until we could afford to get a laminating machine (approximately $200). Without lamination, the symbols are not as durable, so you will have to replace them more often.

To prepare the sheets that hold the symbols, laminate a blank page the size of the notebook or other device you will use for your child's planner. I use the cheapest card stock I can find. You could also use glossy paper for these pages, but it is not economical to do that. Attach strips of Velcro with enough space between rows so there is plenty of room for the symbols to be attached and to be removed easily by your child when he finishes an activity.

The cover you choose for the planner will depend on how your child will use the planner. If he is going to carry it with him, you don't want it to be too cumbersome. You can just make a laminated cover sheet and spiral bind the planner. Billy Ray likes to have something with handles. He uses a Day-Timer planner notebook. It has a big pocket that I put a label on for symbols after he is finished with them. A zippered notebook for students works fine too.

You will also need a notebook to hold the symbols when they are not in the planner. A two-inch cheap notebook works great. You can even use a notebook your child used for school in the past but doesn't use anymore.

I prepared labels for the lower right-hand corner of the same sheets I used for the planner pages. The labels were for the various types of symbols I planned to use. Here are a few examples:

- Home activities (this would include life skills, chores, etc.)
- Leisure activities (these might be at home or in the community—Boardmaker has symbols for McDonald's and other businesses, or you can take a picture of your child's favorite restaurant, bowling alley, etc.)
- School-related activities
- Community activities (this page is for the symbols you make for places your child goes in the community that might not be leisure-related—for example your church, the grocery store, etc.)

- Professionals (this page includes symbols for her doctor, therapist, or other professionals whom she will see from time to time. You might also include the beautician who cuts her hair, her favorite lab technician, etc.)
- Family (this could be pictures of family members whom you will go visit or who will come to visit you; they could include pictures of Grandma's house, etc.)

Activity Visuals

When I started training Billy Ray on his routine, I created the visuals using digital pictures I took of every step of an activity. Eventually he had an activity down pat so that he didn't need to refer to the visual each time. After I had him on a routine, using one symbol for each activity in the communication planner worked fine. After the visuals were no longer useful to Billy Ray, I discovered that I could still use the visuals. They are a great training tool for caregiving assistants. It helps them remember the sequence of steps in an activity.

The "Feeding the Horse" visual (see appendix figure 2) is the first of the activity visuals I did. Billy Ray did not really need a visual because he knew the steps for this task. I wanted him to start on a successful note.

I was excited at the new method I had learned for communicating with Billy Ray. I had no idea that later it would demonstrate to the IEP team that Billy Ray was able to do certain tasks so independently. This was a turning point in getting the team to recognize that Billy Ray was capable of more than he was being challenged with in school.

I prepared one visual for every activity that requires more than one step. I wanted him to have as much success as possible, so I first did visuals for the activities that he already had the highest degree of independence doing. Then we did visuals for new activities we wanted to teach him. There are samples of the various visuals on my website.

Picture Schedules

Picture schedules can be created in computer spreadsheets or tables. They could also be handwritten. Pictures can be inserted into the computer file and the schedules printed out. You can also laminate the schedule and attach Velcro in one column and place a symbol for the activity right on the schedule. This enables your child to remove the symbol and place it in a "done" box when finished. Additionally, he can hold the symbol in his hand when you are announcing the activity.

APPENDIX FIGURE 2   The "Feeding the Horse" visual.

Billy Ray Feeds His Horses Every Day

First Billy Ray gives his horses a can full of grain in their feeders. Then he pushes the hay cart out of the barn. He throws the hay over the fence into the pasture so Baby can get to it. Then he turns the cart around and pushes it back into the barn next to the piles of hay. Billy Ray takes good care of his horses.

Appendix figure 3 is a sample of a picture schedule without as much detail. Depending on your child's response, this may be enough without the detailed schedule for communication. It acts like an appointment schedule from a planner adults might use.

Tip: Recurring schedules can be put in a three-ring binder with page protectors. Some children seem to need to check items off. If so, place the schedules in page protectors that can be written on with dry-erase markers.

Appendix figure 4 is a sample of a picture schedule done in an Excel spreadsheet. It is longer and has much more detail. If your child needs to have an exact sequence, this would work better than the shorter version.

SAMPLE DOCUMENTS

Here are samples of documents I have experimented with for Billy Ray. Some may be helpful in advocating for your child. Others may be more than you need. Adapt to whatever is helpful for you and your child.

Routine Tracking Forms

Appendix figure 5 on page 198 is a sample of an easy routine tracking form you can make to track things such as sleep, bowel movements (if constipation is an issue), appetite, etc. Add whatever things you and the doctor are monitoring. This makes it quicker to get these facts onto the summary for the doctor. You can make a blank tracking form with pen and paper or on your computer and make copies as needed.

Appendix figure 6 on page 199 is a combination of the tracking data for one day (on the top) and journal entries. If you generally have quite a bit to write for your child every day, this might be easiest for you. You would have one page for every day.

Summary Forms

Appendix figure 7 on page 200 is a sample summary for Billy Ray from 2002. Note that the information could be used for either the psychiatrist or pediatrician. Columns can be modified for any item that is significant for your child. I was trying to include enough detail in this summary to demonstrate to the psychiatrist that the medication was making him sleep too much and not reducing the aggression during his waking hours.

I prefer to do these summaries on spreadsheets in landscape format because

(text continued on page 198)

APPENDIX FIGURE 3   Sample picture schedule—less detail.

Time	Visual of Activity	What	Where (Place Activity Occurs)
5:00	Insert digital picture, hand-drawn picture, or software symbol of activity	Take pills	Insert digital picture, hand-drawn picture, or software symbol of room where activity occurs—bedroom
5:05	Insert digital picture, hand-drawn picture, or software symbol of activity	Go to bathroom	Insert digital picture, hand-drawn picture, or software symbol of room where activity occurs—bathroom
	Insert digital picture, hand-drawn picture, or software symbol of activity	Wash hands	Insert digital picture, hand-drawn picture, or software symbol of room where activity occurs—bathroom
	Insert digital picture, hand-drawn picture, or software symbol of activity	Brush teeth	Insert digital picture, hand-drawn picture, or software symbol of room where activity occurs—bathroom
5:15	Insert digital picture, hand-drawn picture, or software symbol of activity	Get dressed	Insert digital picture, hand-drawn picture, or software symbol of room where activity occurs—bedroom
6:10	Insert digital picture, hand-drawn picture, or software symbol of activity	Put coat on and get backpack	Insert digital picture, hand-drawn picture, or software symbol of room where activity occurs—dining room
6:15	Insert digital picture, hand-drawn picture, or software symbol of activity	Feed horses	Insert digital picture, hand-drawn picture, or software symbol of place where activity occurs—barn
6:30	Insert digital picture, hand-drawn picture, or software symbol of activity	Listen to radio in Mom's van	Insert digital picture, hand-drawn picture, or software symbol of place where activity occurs—van at bus stop

APPENDIX FIGURE 4 Sample picture schedule—spreadsheet—more detail.

Before School Schedule

Symbol	When	Activity	Procedure	Comments
Insert symbol for "waking up"	Step 1	Wake him up.	Take dog (his service dog) into his room, help him to stroke her fur to wake up calmly.	
Insert symbol for "toilet"	Step 2	Take him to the toilet.	Cue him by saying, "It's time to go to the bathroom."	If he refuses this process after a few trials, move on to the next activities and return to this one.
Insert symbol for "wash hands"	Step 3	Wash hands and face.	Assist as needed with the process, including washing hands.	
Insert symbol for "take pills"	Step 4	Take morning medications.	Try to get him to come to the table to take pills. If he refuses, bring pills to him.	If he refuses to take his medications, go on to the next activity and start the cues for taking pills again.
Insert symbol for "check planner"	Step 5	Go over symbols with him so he knows what his day is going to be like.	Bring planner to him, either at the table (if he came to the table for his pills) or to his bedroom.	If he has an appointment that day or some special event, try to have the symbol and/or a social story prepared to explain to him what to expect from the event.

		Open to the page that you have placed the symbols for the activities he will be doing between then and school day. Alternatively, you could place the planner's symbols in sequence together.		
		Discuss his schedule with him.		
Step 6	Fix breakfast together.	Billy Ray will wash his hands.	Insert symbol for "breakfast"	
		Billy Ray will get the frying pan from the cupboard and hand to Mom.		
		Mom will get eggs from the refrigerator and break them into a bowl.		
		Billy Ray will place left hand on side of bowl and stir eggs with his right hand.		
		Billy Ray will spray cooking spray in the frying pan and set the pan on the burner.		
		Mom will turn on the burner.		

(continues)

APPENDIX FIGURE 4 Continued.

Before School Schedule

Symbol	When	Activity	Procedure	Comments
			Billy Ray will put clean placements on the table	
			Mom and Billy Ray will count forks and spoons together.	
			Billy Ray will put one fork on each placemat.	
			Billy Ray will put one spoon on each placemat.	
	Step 7	Billy Ray will eat breakfast.	Billy Ray will eat and then put his plate in the sink.	
Insert symbol for "get dressed"	Step 8	Billy Ray takes a bath and dresses for the day.	Billy Ray will get a beach towel from linen closet and spread on his bed while Mom gathers needed lotions, etc. and lays out on his bed.	
			Billy Ray will use the toilet while Mom gets the bathwater ready.	
			Billy Ray will take his clothes off and put them in the hamper.	

Billy Ray will hold the railing on the tub in his left hand and Mom's hand in his right hand and get into the tub. He will let go of Mom's right hand.				
Billy Ray will get washcloth wet and wring it out (Mom's hand over his hand) and wash his face and neck.				
Mom will wash his back.				
Billy Ray will wash his body.				
Mom will fold washcloth and Billy Ray will put it over his eyes.				
Mom will shampoo his hair.				
Mom will dry Billy Ray's hair and face with towel.				
Billy Ray will pull the lever to let the water out of the tub and stand up.				
Billy Ray will hold the railing and Mom's hand and step out.				

(continues)

APPENDIX FIGURE 4 Continued.

Before School Schedule

Symbol	When	Activity	Procedure	Comments
			Mom will dry back, arms, chest, and legs then hand towel to Billy Ray to dry private parts.	
			Mom will wrap towel around Billy Ray and put his slippers on him.	
			They will go to Billy Ray's room and Billy Ray will lay on the bed.	
			Mom will put lotion on his back and medicine on any skin irritations.	
			Billy Ray will put underwear on.	
			Mom will put lotion on Billy Ray's feet and put his socks on.	
			Billy Ray will put pants and shirt on, then Mom will fasten.	

				Mom will set left shoe next to left foot and right next to right foot and Billy Ray will put them on.
Insert symbol for "brush teeth"	Step 9	Billy Ray will brush his teeth, shave, and comb hair.		Billy Ray holds the toothbrush and Mom puts her hand over Billy Ray's hand to guide him while brushing his teeth.
				Mom hands Billy Ray a paper cup with water. Billy Ray takes a swallow to rinse his mouth. Then Billy Ray spits the water in the sink and throws the paper cup away.
Insert symbol for "shave" if desired				Billy Ray holds the electric razor in his hand. Mom puts her hand over Billy Ray's hand to guide him while shaving.
				Mom pours aftershave in Billy Ray's hand. He rubs his hands together and then puts the aftershave on his face.

APPENDIX FIGURE 5   Sample routine tracking form.

Date	Sleep —Day	Routine Meds Time Given	PRN Meds	Appetite	Bowels Moved	Sleep —Night
		AM Lunch Dinner Bedtime		Brkfast: Lunch: Dinner:		
		AM Lunch Dinner Bedtime		Brkfast: Lunch: Dinner:		
		AM Lunch Dinner Bedtime		Brkfast: Lunch: Dinner:		

Note: you can add seizures or other things you are monitoring in addition to or instead of noted items.

I am able to do it on fewer pages and the columns don't run as long. It can also be handwritten, as long as it is clear.

Abbreviated History of Development, Behavior, and Treatment

This history helps in so many ways. When you are asked a question that you don't recall the answer to, it is all right there. When the doctor suggests a medication that you think you may have tried with poor results, you can review the history to be sure before starting it for your child. It is also available as history in the event that you are no longer able to take care of your child.

Appendix figure 8 on page 207 is a partial example from Billy Ray's history. Note that I have deleted some of the medication names because I do not want to encourage or discourage use based on Billy Ray's experiences.

Task List

When you are sitting in a meeting discussing your child's abilities, it is sometimes hard to demonstrate verbally what your child can do. Having a list of what he does at home and the degree of assistance he needs helps demonstrate your point and is usually better received. It can also be used with caregivers to teach the level of assistance they should provide your child. Appendix figure 9 on page 209 is a partial sample task list.

APPENDIX FIGURE 6 Sample combination form.

Notes for _____, 20___

Date	Sleep —Day	Routine Meds Time Given	PRN Meds	Appetite	Bowels Moved	Sleep —Night
		AM Lunch Dinner Bedtime		Brkfast: Lunch: Dinner:		

Sample Comparison of Functioning at Various Points

The purpose of doing this comparison is to demonstrate to the professionals how your child has improved or deteriorated between two points in time. Sometimes the comparison could be done to show the improvement or deterioration during a medication trial.

Appendix figure 10 on page 212 is a sample of a comparison I did to show the deterioration Billy Ray experienced between the seizures at fourteen years old and a period nearly three years later.

Transitional Plan

The goals included in the transitional plan will depend largely on your child's age and developmental stage. If you start too early, you may not know what you can realistically expect him to achieve. On the other hand, if you wait too long to start planning, needed skills may be substantially unachievable.

(text continued on page 210)

APPENDIX FIGURE 7   Sample summary.

Date	Sleep (Hrs.)	Events/Stressors, Etc.	Aggression Degree/Toward	Refusal	PRN Meds or Change in Meds
6/12/02	9.5 night sleep (woke up once)	District office chores, long visit with psychiatrist.	2 mod—Staff, 1 mod—Mom, 1 mod to severe—hitting Mom & staff, threw dish and running at restaurant	Very tired, not wanting to get out of car to see doctor.	
6/13/02	11 hours night (woke up twice), 3.5 hrs. day sleep	Did chores, ran errands.			
6/14/02	10 hours night (woke up once)	District office chores, McDonald's, home chores, and session with therapist.			
6/15/02	10 hours night (woke up twice), 3 hours in two daytime naps	Very loud but co-operative. Got agitated a couple of times but responded well to behavioral intervention, including Gator rides on property.			
6/16/02	9 hours night (woke up once), short nap during church	Church in a.m., very very well behaved but sleepy.	1 Mod to severe punch—Mom driving home		

Date	Sleep	Behavior			
6/17/02	9 hours night (woke up once), 3.5 hours	Loud and agitated but redirectable. Did chores at home, district office, and lunch at restaurant.			Dumped out first attempt at prune juice/lactulose; drank second.
6/18/02	12 hours night (awake 3 times), 4 hours day	Loud and bouncy, appeared to rapidly cycle—tired, then bouncy, then falling asleep.			
6/19/02	14 hours night sleep (awake twice)	It took two hours of trying to wake him up before we got him up. Loud and bouncing. Gator ride helped.			
6/20/02	13 hours night sleep (awake once)	Cooperative with farm chores and normal routine, played with Baby Doll, Gator rides.			
6/21/02	10 hours—woke up, took pills, and fell asleep for another 3.75 hours.	Participated in routine activities at district office and home chores.			
6/22/02	14 hours night sleep (woke up once)	Very noisy and loud but redirectable.	2 Mod—Mom		
6/23/02	13.5 hours, 2.25 hours day sleep	Seemed very tired but trying to cooperate with activities.			

(continues)

APPENDIX FIGURE 7 Continued.

Date	Sleep (Hrs.)	Events/Stressors, Etc.	Aggression Degree/Toward	Refusal	PRN Meds or Change in Meds
6/24/02	13 hours night sleep (woke up twice), slept in car plus 1 hr 45 min in 2 naps	At times bouncing and loud. Appeared to be rapidly cycling. NOTE THAT IN THE MIDDLE OF TALKING TO THERAPIST, HIS ABILITY TO FOCUS CHANGED, HE SWITCHED FROM BEING HAPPY/ COOPERATIVE TO AGITATED AND THEN FELL INTO A FAIRLY DEEP SLEEP INSTANTLY. Was able to wake up and participate in his district office and home chores.			Reduced Trazodone to 50mg. per night per psych nurse.
6/25/02	12.25 hours night sleep (woke up once), various naps in the car driving	Noisy but cooperative. Two incidents of incontinence while going to shopping center (very rare for him).			
6/26/02	13 hours night sleep (woke up once)	Cooperative with farm chores and normal routine, but loud and bouncing.			

Date	Sleep	Behavior	Notes
6/27/02	10.25 hours night sleep (woke up twice), 3.25 hours day sleep	Sleepy, noisy, growling. Participated in some of his activities but seemed tired.	Refusing bathroom and some chores but eventually did cooperate.
6/28/02	12 hours night (woke up once), 4 hours day	Very happy participating in his district office activities. Staff noted that he was smiling and waving hi and goodbye.	
6/29/02	14 hours night sleep (awake once), 5 hours day sleep	Woke up at 8 a.m. Cooperative in activities. About 11 a.m. his behavior became manic, then he fell asleep suddenly and slept five hours. When I tried to wake him up a few times, he either didn't respond or raised his head but fell right back to sleep.	
6/30/02	12 hours night, 4 hours day	Woke up at 7:30 a.m. and followed a.m. routine until time to choose clothes before bath,	Missed noon medications due to sleep.

(continues)

APPENDIX FIGURE 7 Continued.

Date	Sleep (Hrs.)	Events/Stressors, Etc.	Aggression Degree/Toward	Refusal	PRN Meds or Change in Meds
		seemed too tired to choose clothes and appeared stuck in that decision. Sat in chair and fell asleep following what appeared to be mania, followed by what appeared to be confusion. Attempts to wake him up after an hour failed. Once awake he cooperated with eating, toileting, etc.			
7/1/02	14 hours	Appeared to be cycling between smiling and happy to loud and bouncing.			Decreased Trazodone per psych nurse.
7/2/02	13.5 hours night sleep (woke up once)	Fairly calm and co-operative but seemed tired all day. Didn't actually fall asleep during day but appeared on the verge of it most of the day.			
7/3/02	13 hours night sleep, 3.75 hours day sleep	Awake at 8 a.m. Co-operative until time to choose clothes, went to master suite to take bath			Missed lunch and lunch medications.

		and then ran around the house naked. Seemed to get stuck in decision of what to wear, was confused, then fell asleep. Unable to wake him up.	
7/4/02	12 hours night sleep, 3.5 hours day sleep	Basically repeat of previous events where he cooperates, becomes confused, then falls asleep for 3–5 hours during the day.	Missed lunch but got medications late.
7/5/02	9 hours night sleep, 5.25 hours day sleep.	Woke up at 5:30 a.m., took medications but fell back to sleep and slept 5.25 hours. Cooperative with activities after he finally woke up for second time.	

(continues)

APPENDIX FIGURE 7 Continued.

Date	Sleep (Hrs.)	Events/Stressors, Etc.	Aggression Degree/Toward	Refusal	PRN Meds or Change in Meds
7/6/02	12 hours night sleep (woke up once), 5 hours day sleep	Woke up at 9:30 hyper and agitated, didn't eat well, confusion, appeared stuck. Back to sleep 2 hours after woke up and slept 5 hours. Unable to wake him. Agitated at bedtime and aggressive	2 severe punches to Mom		1 mg. Ativan at 10:30 p.m. for aggression.
7/7/02	14 hours night sleep (woke up once), 4 hours day sleep	Repeat of previous days: got up, started routine, and fell asleep just before bath. I DID NOTE SOME EYE FLUTTERING AND CONFUSION JUST BEFORE FALLING ASLEEP THIS TIME. Monitored breathing closely and attempted to wake up after 1 hour but unable to do so.			

APPENDIX FIGURE 8   Sample abbreviated history of development, behavior, and treatment.

Age	Behavior/Symptom/Event	Diagnosis	Treatment
15 months to 4 yrs.	Placed with us, following foster care and a failed adoption, cute Down's baby. Rapidly gained skills, terrible twos. Head Start and multihandicapped preschool.	Down syndrome, recurrent ear infections, undernourished	Antibiotics, tubes in his ears
4–5 yrs.	School complaints of hyperactivity. Difficult to keep focused at home.	ADHD	Stimulant
5–9 yrs.	First manic episode triggered by Dad's car wreck then grief for a special pickup truck. Mania, including running, throwing, dumping displays at school. Dr. Ron called in near 7 yrs.	Down syndrome, ADHD, bipolar—manic/depression	[list of drugs tried by psychiatrist]
9–13 yrs.	Reasonably stable, high functioning. Very socially confident and appropriate. Difficult to get to sleep and hard to get up for school, tardy a lot. Some cycling. Dad died at 11 yrs. Wanted a new Dad ASAP. Signs of puberty at 12 years.	Same	[list of drugs tried by psychiatrist]
	Just past 13 years, we met present stepfather, moved to farming community. Mainstreamed with one-on-one aide. Self-esteem and functioning very highest ever. Sleep problems still present.	Same	Added _____ for sleep

(continues)

APPENDIX FIGURE 8 Continued.

Age	Behavior/Symptom/Event	Diagnosis	Treatment
13½ to 14½ yrs.	Placed in more restrictive classroom. Teacher constantly complained about hyper behavior. Finally changed medications. Larry made a list of behaviors at home—Dr. S. said normal for his developmental age.	Same	Tegratol discontinued due to blood count; seizure caused from reaction to [drug for ADHD]
	So manic he would come out of his room throwing dirty clothes, hangers, or books; unsafe to drive with him—would take shoes off and throw at driver. Silly and giggly during negative behaviors.	No change	No regular medications
	Hospitalized for evaluation at adolescent psych unit. On discharge, he was alternating between being a zombie and a wild man; stopped eating—lost 16 lbs. in 2 months, more out of school than in. Symptoms of autism began appearing within three months following seizures—most notably with communication problems and hesitance to be touched.		Mood stabilizer started

APPENDIX FIGURE 9   Sample task list.

Task	Level of Assistance Needed	Comments
Make bed, including changing bottom sheet (he does not use top sheet)	Assistant puts on one corner of fitted sheet and he puts on the rest of the sheet. He occasionally needs additional assistance with second corner. After putting sheet on, cue him to smooth wrinkles out and him pull it tight. Cue him to put the comforter and pillows on and smooth them out.	
Vacuum bedroom carpet	Assistant gets vacuum ready and turns it on. He tends to get stuck in one spot. If he continues on the same spot for a couple of tries put your hand over his hand and guide him to keep moving to another spot.	
Empty garbage	Needs help getting the bag out of the garbage can. Needs help with the front door and rarely with the lid on the outside garbage can. Needs someone to go with him so he doesn't wander away.	
Wash sink and wipe counters in his bathroom	Assistant holds hand over Billy Ray's hand on the cleaning spray to spray sink and counters (Billy Ray tends to use it as a gun or spray too much on counter).	

(continues)

APPENDIX FIGURE 9 Continued.

Task	Level of Assistance Needed	Comments
Unload dishwasher	Ensure adequate hand washing. Remove sharp knives before starting process with Billy Ray. He has a high degree of independence in this task unless he can't reach area the object belongs in. Occasionally he will need to be cued where to put things.	
Put dirty dishes in the dishwasher	Billy Ray is less independent in loading than unloading the dishwasher. In order to avoid needing to rearrange items, put your hand over his hand or let him give you the dishes from the sink. He can put silverware in basket independently.	Work gradually on having him learn to put glasses in the rack correctly.

Here is a partial sample. Obviously it is incomplete but will give you an idea of what should be included.

TRANSITIONAL PLAN

1. Residential Goals:

   To live with the highest degree of independence appropriate for his level of functioning at age 18–20. Potential options:

   A. Independent living in apartment with SILP trainer and Mom checking in to ensure well-being

   B. Semi-independent apartment program with on-site supervision always available for assistance when needed

   C. Group home, such as _____

2. Vocational Goals:

   To explore various job tasks to find comfort level, interest, and ability to perform in positions such as:

      A. Janitorial crew

      B. Dishwasher at restaurant

      C. Sheltered workshop

3. Academic Goals:

      To ascertain what can be reasonably achieved while still in school to add quality to his life and provide skills for transition needs.

      A. IEP goals will be broken down into steps to master skills necessary to achieve above residential and vocational goals

Note: Although some skills can be acquired through work with the SILP trainer, the basic skills listed in appendix figure 11 must be present for this goal to be prudent.

Many things could be added to this. The idea is to take a general look at how realistic this plan is. Additionally, it opens the discussion in IEP meetings about what skills your child needs to acquire in school to realistically expect to achieve his or her goals. You can also take notes or use the sample format for these additional goals in the transitional plan.

APPENDIX FIGURE 10   Comparison of functioning/skills.

Functioning at Age 10–14 Years	Functioning at Age 19 (4½ Yrs Following Medication Reaction–Induced Seizures)
Able to dress himself independently.	Clothes are put on backward if he is even able to get them on by himself at all.
Able to be trusted to go across the hall from Mom's office to the bathroom by himself and return.	Can't be left alone.
Trustworthy to sit at restaurant table while Mom went to the bathroom.	Can't be left alone.
Played quietly in Mom's office while she worked, attended meetings, and visited clients with Mom. Totally trustworthy.	Too noisy to be involved in work-related activities with Mom. Can't be trusted alone long enough for Mom or caregiver to go to the bathroom.
Went to very nice restaurants with Mom for business meetings or business/social contacts. A joy for all to be around.	Desperately wants to go out but too noisy and unable to sit long enough to even allow Mom to finish her meal. May throw things, pass gas, choke, and yell the entire time.
Could choose menu items and order, being understood for the most part even by strange server.	Has difficulty choosing just his own drink. Speech content and articulation difficult to understand.
Couldn't get him to eat enough.	Doesn't seem to know when he is full and will eat and eat until stopped.
Loved to play in his room or outside independently, sometimes for hours. Could always be trusted to be where he was supposed to be and come when called. We had to beg him to be out in the living areas with us. Went outside to feed the dogs independently.	Can't stay focused on anything—sometimes not even for 15 seconds. Has no interest in playing independently and can't be trusted outside or he takes off down the road. Must have one-on-one supervision to avoid certain behaviors and make him feel comfortable.
Able to do many household chores, some independently.	Needs assistance with everything and able to do very few chores, even with supervision.
Proud of his accomplishments.	Low self-esteem.
Redirectable, even when manic.	Often not redirectable at all.
Eager to please, compliant.	Easily agitated, frustrated, and defiant.

APPENDIX FIGURE 11 Skills necessary for independent living with SILP trainer.

Skill/Ability	Subskill Needed	IEP Goals
Ability to get help	Telephone skills	Number recognition
		911 use
		Ability to find phone number from list or phone book
		Basic operating of a telephone and/or answering machine
Ability to medicate self	Able to tell time or understand some type of alarm system for when to take the medications	Time-telling skills
Basic self-care skills	Proper hygiene	
	Basic cooking skills	Simple meal preparation, especially breakfast and making a sack lunch
		Use of a microwave and range
	Basic housekeeping skills	This may or may not be offered in school programs—IEP goals would depend on whether there was a life-skills program in your child's school
Basic home safety	Locking doors and windows	
	Knowledge of who is allowed entrance to his home	Stranger-danger program
	Fire safety	Avoiding fires
		Training in use of fire extinguisher for small fires
		Concept of when to get the fire extinguisher and when to get out of the building

INDEX